Endorsements

"We all face challenges in our lives that can seem insurmountable. We may feel hopeless and overwhelmed by the complexity of life in a world that seems to be spinning out of control. How would your life be different if you realized and embraced that within every challenge is a gift and a blessing?

"*Remembrances* offers a diametrically opposed perspective on the world and our relationships to God and others. Our thoughts and actions can bring us everything we desire. We are constantly connected to each other and to God. Our apparent isolation is just an illusion. Karl Morgan reminds us, if we have faith in God and in ourselves, we can fulfill our destiny to love unconditionally and experience true happiness in our lives."

Sharon Lund, DD, author of
There Is More . . . 18 Near-Death Experiences

"*Remembrances* is a thoughtful, insightful, and inspiring book filled with many great lessons. Karl Morgan lifts the veil of mystery to ancient, spiritual truth as he combines contemporary psychology with ageless wisdom. Within these pages you will realize how close you are to God and each other and that will give you hope. This is a powerful read."

Judy Winkler, author of
Get Unstuck: Live with Ease

REMEMBRANCES

REMEMBRANCES:

Choose to Be Happy and Embrace the Possibilities

Karl Morgan

Sacred Life Publishers™
www.sacredlife.com
Printed in United States of America

REMEMBRANCES:
Choose to Be Happy and Embrace the Possibilities

Copyright © 2012 by Karl Morgan

All rights reserved. No part of this book may be used or reproduced by any means, graphic, electronic, or mechanical, including photocopying, recording, taping, or by any information storage retrieval system without the written permission of the publisher except in the case of brief quotations embodied in critical articles and reviews.

Remembrances may be purchased or ordered through booksellers or at SacredLife.com.

ISBN: 0982646194
ISBN: 978-0-9826461-9-9
Library of Congress Control Number: 2012944994

The information, ideas, and suggestions in this book are not intended as a substitute for professional advice. Before following any suggestions contained in this book, consult your physician or mental health professional. Neither the author nor the publisher shall be liable or responsible for any loss or damage allegedly arising as a consequence of your use or application of any information or suggestions in this book.

Cover and text design: Miko Radcliffe at Drawingacrowd.net
Cover Photo NasaImages.org "Happy Sweet Sixteen"
Hubble Telescope

Sacred Life Publishers™
www.sacredlife.com
Printed in United States of America

Dedication

This book is dedicated to the love of my life, my wonderful wife Aida. She has loved me and been my rock for more than twenty years, helping me to be a better person. Her calm guidance, wisdom and affection helped me recognize the haughtiness in the original manuscript and give the book a warmer, more joyful tone. Because of her, I am better able to tell this story in an open and loving way, which was my goal all along.

Her Jewish faith also opened my eyes to other perspectives on life and the nature of existence. There have been many incredible teachers over the course of history who have taught us that our spiritual existence is reality and to focus on that rather than the noise and commotion around us.

Thanks, sweetie-pie!

Contents

Endorsements i

Dedication vii

Foreword xi

Chapter 1 Before This Life Chapter 1

Chapter 2 Finding Your Heart's Desire 5

Chapter 3 Believe and Be Happy 11

Chapter 4 Faith, Abundance and Success 15

Chapter 5 Responsibility 17

Chapter 6 The End of Fear 19

Chapter 7 Three Honorable Men 21

Chapter 8 Words to the Wise 45

Chapter 9 The Lessons 63

Chapter 10 Our Nobility 95

Chapter 11 The Course of Enlightenment 101

Chapter 12 Lives 105

Chapter 13 Words to Consider about Toa 107

Chapter 14 Closing Thoughts 109

About the Author 113

Foreword

Take heart! The world is here to help you be happy and take you toward enlightenment. The events of your life are your lessons, and your reactions are your exams. Best of all, no one fails. We all proceed at our own pace, and that pace is perfectly in line with the desires of God.

The end result of life is death, as the classroom bell sounds at the end of the day. While the end is sad for the schoolhouse and the teachers left behind, classes will resume in the morning. Upon graduation all doubt will be resolved and you will have truly learned.

Chapter 1

Before This Life Chapter

Wherein the author defines how he came to meet the student.

Many years ago, just before you began this lifetime, you chose this universe to be the vehicle for your experience. At that moment you knew the total truth about this universe, accepted it, and even yearned for the experience to begin. Then your soul was free, and being free was able to choose among an infinite number of possible Experience-Universes for its education.

You took the Experience Catalog home with you, and spent the better part of a day, or week, or year analyzing the possibilities and calculating the benefits of each Experience-Universe. Somehow (probably through incredible insight) you chose this Earth-Time Universe.

Then you filled out the enclosed postage-paid card, and submitted your request. Upon due consideration of a higher authority, your request was approved, and notification was sent to you that your Experience-Universe would be available at such and such time. In the intervening period, you straightened out your affairs, such as putting the dog in the kennel and stopped the milk deliveries.

At the appointed hour, you went to the Experience-Universe Initiation Center and waited for your turn. All around you were the anxious faces of others about to enter the same universe, or some other, and the joyous faces of those who had just returned. How your mind had turned then. "Were they happy to have had the experience, or were they just happy to have it be over? Well, no matter, I have chosen the Earth-Time universe from many prior happy experiences, and the happy or sad experiences of others will not deter me from the joyous fulfillment of my destiny." You were so wise!

You were ushered into the briefing room at the appointed hour. You were amazed at how many of your friends were there. Of course, you had spared no expense to convince many of them to come and share the experience, but still you were overjoyed at how many friends they had brought along. Somewhere in that crowd was me. You busily greeted all the souls there, greeting old friends, thanking others for being there, and meeting many souls for the first time. That day, I told you that I would help you remember all of this when you needed it, but you were certain that it would not come to that.

We were all told to sit down in the very comfortable Experience-Loungers, and in doing so began to relax more completely. Gradually, our eyes became heavier and heavier, until at last... we felt... that we... just... could not... stay ... awake... any... longer...

Then the entire universe turned upside down. You were truly alone... and falling. You could feel the cold of the outside air on your delicate skin. It was so strange to feel confined to that shell of skin again. Suddenly, hands were all over you... wiping what? Ah yes, blood and fluid from all over your body. Touch was another strange sensation to remember. You had forgotten it, and it was nice, very sensuous, yet isolating at the same time.

You began to plan. "Good! I made it back to the Earth-Time Universe again. I am ready to do it right this time. No more of this forgetting stuff. Too many lifetimes have been wasted through failure to recognize that I already have had most of these experiences before. But now, I remember it all, and will use the past as a bridge. I can start out at the point where I ended the last time." Yes, a perfect experience was planned, but then what happened?

"Oh my goodness, I forgot to breathe. These people must be worried. I guess that means I'm not fully alive yet . . . oh no . . . that swat is not necessary. I can cry."

And a baby cried. And in his tears, all the truths of ten thousand lifetimes were lost. Thus began the journey of you . . . who you are today . . . and who you will be tomorrow.

The time has come for me to fulfill the promise I made in the Experience-Initiation Center. I hope that my memory does not fail me too utterly. One of us has to remember, and as I have not yet heard from you, it must be up to me. Let us begin.

Chapter 2

Finding Your Heart's Desire

If you can remember one thing from these words, I hope it is that this universe of experience is yours and yours alone. If you can believe that, you will find it much easier to accept the wonders the universe offers to fulfill your desires. Forgetting this truth has led to most, if not all of mankind's problems.

It is not easy to accept that we are responsible for what is happening in our lives. It seems more convenient to place blame elsewhere, on God, on fate, or other people. Yet, this is a big mistake. By placing blame on others, we are accepting our inability to change what is happening and to improve our lives.

If we believe that we are impotent in this life, then we feel that we have no control over the future. If events in our lives are out of our control, how can we be responsible for what happens next? If we are not responsible, then there is truly nothing we can do to improve our lot. From that moment, we begin to believe that life is a battle that we cannot win.

Yet, in that time before you began this Earth-Time universe experience, you knew that you were choosing all of this, and that was exactly what you wanted. How do you regain that knowledge? Let us continue this train of thought.

All of the events of your life have brought you to this exact moment. That is plainly true because you are here, reading these words. Think back for a moment, and remember all the things that have happened in your life that have made you who you are today. Doubtlessly, you are beginning to compile a quite a list.

We each have made thousands of decisions throughout our lives. Any of those could have changed our future. The sum of all those choices brought us together now. You think that is just coincidence? Nonsense! For any number of reasons, you have chosen or been driven down a path which led to this moment, and you have come this way to learn, or re-learn something from what is written on these pages. That is no coincidence. Everything has happened in accordance with your heart's desire.

What is your heart's desire? Probably you are yearning to know the reality of your life. Why are you here? How can you be happy? Why is life so unfair? Of course, you already know the answers to these and a million more questions, but you have forgotten them. Why do you refuse to remember them? The answers give you too much responsibility.

It is too easy to allow the power in our lives to fly away to someone else or to God or Nature. Once that power is lost, we are no longer guilty for the problems that confront us. Without guilt, we can complain and whine about our lives and pray for salvation from the Earth, and envy those with more money and more happiness. In our heart, we can be sure that we are not responsible for these difficulties.

We really are responsible. We choose our adventures, successes, and failures. Not only does this mean that you have created this mess on your own, but you also have the power to make your life better. No one can take that power from you. Only you can give it away. This is the most difficult lesson to learn in life. Perhaps there is a less harsh way of looking at it?

Imagine for a second that the course of your life is totally out of your control, as if the physical world did exist. Then you, as a speck of dust on a speck of a planet on the edge of a minor galaxy in the middle of eternal space, you are totally helpless. The

Finding Your Heart's Desire

eternal course of the universe will direct the events of your life, and you are powerless to change them.

On the other hand, imagine a universe which does not exist, except in your desire to use it to learn and be happy. In that universe, you are able to control events that occur in every corner, and most importantly, you can control your destiny.

Now you have two possible versions of your universe. Perhaps either could be true. Does it matter which one is correct? Not if you choose to believe that you can control your universe. Let me explain. If the universe is out of your control, but you think you can control it, you may succeed in improving your life by fighting and working hard for the things that matter to you. If the universe is out of your control, and you know and accept that, then you stand to gain nothing other than what random chance chooses to deliver.

If the universe is of your creation and you know it, then the sky is the limit. You can have and do anything, and be truly happy in your experience of it. If this is your universe and you deny it and allow the illusion to control you, you will have lost the opportunity to experience the things you came here to enjoy. When you awaken in your Experience-Lounger, you will remember and feel sorry for the waste of time and the lost experience.

The bottom line is that taking control of your life is always the better course. It will always make you feel better about your circumstances and may well allow you to have the happiness you richly deserve. When we wake in our Loungers after the experience, you will turn to me and thank me for reminding you. You are quite welcome!

Now that we know the reason you are reading this, and how you have reached this point in life, let us figure out where to go from here. Too often in this Earth-Time universe, we forget that we control our lives and have the power to make our lives as wonderful as we can imagine. Once forgotten, we lose track of the direction in our lives and forget the goals we set out to accomplish.

We need to find the appropriate situation or words to refocus our efforts on the true business of our lives. While analyzing our destinies seems academic and complicated, it is neither. In an illusory universe it is possible to be and do anything. All we have to figure out is "What do we want to do?" Unfortunately, that is tougher than it seems.

First, if you are a living, breathing human being, the odds are that you are not fulfilling your heart's desire. Not that it is impossible; it is very possible, easy actually. The complexity of the experience of life on Earth is a major distraction. Also, other people keep us from finding our paths by telling us their version of the truth and how we should act and behave. How can you tell if you are doing your life's work? If you have to ask that question, you are not. If you have any doubt whether you are doing it, you are not. If you are not happy with yourself and your life, you are not. Pretty simple, yes?

So how do we find our heart's desire, our life's work? That is a much harder question. The real question becomes "What makes me happy?" That is difficult to answer because we are so accustomed to doing what other people want us to do. We are unable to focus on what makes us happy. You and I, and each one of the seven billion humans on this planet are here for a reason. It sounds unlikely, but that reason is to be happy and enjoy our lives. Each of us enjoys life in a different way. Of course, there are similarities, but your experience of the world is different from mine and from every other person's experience. No one else can see through your eyes, or know your sense of touch.

This is a fortunate circumstance, and not coincidental either. We all have deliberately chosen the environment in which we live. We have chosen this particular set of scenes because they allow us to express our heart's desire in the most fulfilling way. That is why we are most happy when we are doing our life's work. Why would I, as a writer, choose to come to a universe to write about these truths if everyone here already knew them and acted upon them? Writing self-help books for advanced souls would be like writing swimming instructions for fish! Instead, I chose to express my beliefs in a universe which needs to hear them.

The same logic will hold for you in the experience of your heart's desire. Those things you wish to bring into your life to improve your life-experience will serve to complement your heart's desire. It is only natural. That bears special emphasis:

> You chose the events of your life to fulfill your heart's desire. You will only be truly happy when you fulfill that desire by going through these events. You decided that these events would make you happy and lead you where you want to go.

This is why so many people seem to have the world at their fingertips and are still unhappy. While they have acquired material possessions, they have not achieved what they came here for and are still searching for something to give meaning to their lives.

Once we remember that we do have a purpose in this life, and accept that we have the responsibility and ability to achieve it, we can begin a path that will lead us to our life's goal, our heart's desire. In summary, the points to remember are:

1. Believing that the universe is unreal is not crucial to your happiness. It is always better to act as if you have control and thereby attempt to improve your life.

2. The situation in which you find yourself is of your choosing. All the so called bad and good events in your life happened for a reason. They brought you to this point where you can change the course of your life for the better.

3. The events of your present are there for a reason. They exist to make your heart's desire better. Only by acknowledging and recognizing your real purpose can you put those events into perspective and enjoy your life.

Accepting that you have a great purpose for your life and taking responsibility for making that happen are the first steps in the fulfillment of your heart's desire. These are the building blocks for finding the path you chose. In these words, I hope you can find the basic realities of the illusory universe and by accepting them; you can be better able to have a full and happy life.

Chapter 3

Believe and Be Happy

Now that you are beginning to recognize your control over the world around you, it is time to work on modifying behaviors. The modification is not for you; it is for the world! You have allowed this universe to become lazy and sluggish and to do its own bidding. Now that you realize that this was your own fault, it is time to start retraining the universe to give you the things you want. This is a touchy subject as it is based on the notion that YOU DESERVE TO HAVE THE THINGS YOU WANT. You must now convince the universe and yourself that this is true. As with a pet, once the universe realizes who is the boss, its training will accelerate.

How do you convince the universe that you are good and worthwhile, and therefore deserving of all the good available in the world? You must act as if it was already so, and then it will be. If you want the world to love you and give you happiness through the fulfillment of your heart's desire, you must love the world and give it happiness by allowing the heart's desires of others to be fulfilled. Imagine for a moment that all the people in the world have special desires that they believe will make their lives worthwhile. Also imagine that the desires of those others were chosen so as to complement your special desires. By your support of those others, your own desires can be better fulfilled.

This sounds somewhat like a sacrifice of your desires to help others. That is only partially true. Your own heart's desire was chosen by you to complement those of the friends around you. Therefore, you will best express love and caring for the universe by fulfilling your own heart's desire. It is important to recognize that some sacrifices will be needed.

> Joan worked for the same company faithfully for many years. Her coworkers came to depend upon Joan heavily, as only she knew all the details which made the company successful. Yet in her heart, Joan felt hollow. She had dreamed of becoming a minister. Joan had learned so much and felt so strongly about her convictions that she felt she would burst if she could not say what she felt inside.
>
> In time, Joan began to study for the ministry, first as an advocate, and finally as the main goal in her life. The more she learned, the more she thirsted to teach. One day, her teachers called upon her and told her that she had completed her course work. With their blessing, she was ordained.
>
> The following day, Joan met with Harry, her boss, and told him that she had been ordained and that the time had come for her to leave the company and to pursue her life's work. "But we need you!" Harry said, "We cannot succeed without your help, and our failure will be your fault!"
>
> Joan's resolve was strong. She left the company and began her ministry. Over the following months, the company suffered gravely. Huge amounts of money were lost and several employees were fired. In their hearts, they all blamed Joan for leaving them.

Joan's ministry suffered as well because people didn't want to hear the truth about control over destiny, and making life better by insisting on the best. The people were unable to believe that they had control over their lives. Through all of the problems, Joan's resolve continued to be strong. In time, her ministry turned around. She found a large, albeit different congregation that wanted to hear the truth for what it was. They learned, became strong and happy, and fulfilled their lives.

The people who had lost their jobs found new jobs, which made them happier. They also realized that Joan was not the cause of the failure of the company. Some of them even joined Joan's congregation. As for the company, it doesn't matter. If the company turned around, it was for the benefit of the remaining workers, who decided that they deserved to have another chance to be happy through the experience of the company. If it failed, it was because all of the employees needed to go elsewhere to find their true selves. Since the company is a thing (a manifestation of the universe) and does not truly live, it was worth sacrificing for the benefit of the people in it.

So it is in all of human experience. We become so accustomed to the aspects that our friends show us that we become alarmed and frightened when they change. In time, we accept the change and eventually see that the change was for the better. All too often, that realization comes only after a large dose of contempt, anger and scorn. This display of resentment is the only thing that keeps many of us from fulfilling our destinies. We spend so much time pleasing others, regardless of our own feelings, that we never even discover what our heart's desires might be. To make things worse, those same important people in our lives are doing the exact same thing. While it may not feel that way to us, they are performing the way they feel we want or expect them to. That means that everyone plays their silly game, and by doing so can waste their lives.

What can we do to stop all this craziness? Just STOP PLAYING GAMES! Express your true self all the time through love and caring. Realize that everyone else is afraid to express reality and is not telling the truth about their feelings either. Try to find out what those true feelings are, and help others express them. Above all, through your ability to express the reality of your soul, learn that you truly do deserve the best in life, and that you can have it too.

Once you begin to feel that maybe you do deserve the good of the world, act as if you already have it. Let it come into your arms and warm and fulfill you. Remember the lesson of Joan the minister. You will not allow yourself to succeed easily. You will probably nearly fail, maybe several times. Yet, through persistence all is gained. You do deserve the best and if you continue to be yourself, expressing the love within you, you will be fulfilled. That is the promise of the universe. If only you could remember that you asked me to remind you of all these truths. Believe and make it so. Have faith, and trust yourself and the hand of God to move together for the betterment of us all.

Chapter 4

Faith, Abundance and Success

I believe in God.

I believe that the physical universe is the perfect and infinite expression of the perfect and infinite God.

I believe in myself.

I believe that I am the perfect and infinite expression of a perfect and infinite God.

Being perfect and infinite, my desires are in line with the wishes of God for me, and available to me considering the infinite resources of the universe. There is no want that I could have which cannot be satisfied because the supply of things is infinite. There is no want that I could have which would conflict with the wants of another, because the plan of God will satisfy each one.

Knowing that the supply of things is infinite, and that my desires are the same as the desires of God for me, I accept into my life all the things that I desire.

Further, I acknowledge that my desires have already been placed in the universe by the Plan of God, and that my only required action is the acceptance of them.

I know that my success in accepting my heart's desires is assured, as these things are part of the Plan of God (of which I am a significant part), have already been placed into the universe by

Remembrances

the Plan of God, and are simply awaiting my acceptance of my abundance.

I am grateful for my abundance, and as I believe, God has made it so. Amen.

Chapter 5

Responsibility

I can remember the disappointments in my life.

I can see them even now, and can feel now what I felt then at the acknowledgement of them.

As I feel them, I feel them gradually fade away into the memories they should be. Their power fades along with the image of them. The pain in my heart and in my soul fades along with their image. They fade, and fade, and fade until they represent nothing.

I can see the current state of my life. I can see why I am happy and why I am sad. I recognize the impact of my past, now forgotten, upon my present, but will start here, today, with a clean slate.

I accept the responsibility for my future. I accept that only I have the ability to make tomorrow better than today. If the winds of fortune blow against me tomorrow, then I will make my life start anew the following day.

I resolve that nothing will sway me from this new direction, for I have learned that no one else will improve my life for me.

All the choices are in my hands, and my new life lays ahead, full of joy and contentment, awaiting only my call. Let it progress according to my hopes. As it is said, so let it be done.

Chapter 6

The End of Fear

Fear is the heavy, barred door that exists between you and the fulfillment of your heart's desire. The bars and chains are cold, blue steel, composed of molecules of self-doubt, apprehension, and uncertainty for the future.

Yet you are resolved to find that goal on the other side of your fear. The other paths of your life have failed, and through your failures have brought you to this door. You know that there can be no turning back as heartbreak lies there. Still, the task at hand is monumental. Each chain and bar you remove is brutally heavy and your heart and muscles feel ready to burst. So many bars, so little strength. Still, your resolve is strong.

So it goes . . . a little progress every day. However, fear is enormous as it has no bounds other than those which are self imposed. Tears stream down your face as your strength wanes and the failures of the past appear more livable, and almost desirable. Maybe it is better to hold that fear rather than risk safety and death? What to do? What to do?

In that hour, your true friends will come and add their strength to yours; and your tears will dry and their love will refresh you for the task ahead. Bar by bar, and chain by chain the task progresses. Though your arms grow weary, your souls are strengthened and you will cast those weights each a thousand miles behind you. By and by, the door will be uncovered. Then you and your friends will push that door with all of your remaining strength until it cracks open slightly. In that moment of near success, two events will occur:

Remembrances

1. The sounds of a million hissing vipers will pour from the blindingly bright interior of your heart's desire. It will be a sound so thunderous that your heart will quake with apprehension.

2. Your friends will say, "The door is now open and your heart's desire waits within. As it is your fear and your heart's desire, we must leave you now." Then they will be gone.

You will remember their faith in you, and your own courage will return. You will continue to push, inch by inch. The sound will rise to that of ten thousand beating drums, and the noise will echo down to your bones, and your soul will shudder with doubt. With your last ounce of strength, love and faith, you will push your fear completely aside, and deafened by the beating sounds, unafraid step in.

In that moment, you will find all of your loved ones inside, cheering and applauding madly and thunderously that their favorite child has joined them. You will look behind and find the hallway darkened, gone forever. Gradually the opening will close, leaving no regrets. Looking at your friends, you will be embraced by their love, with tears of joy in their eyes.

Chapter 7

Three Honorable Men

Three men left their city on a pilgrimage to the mountain temple wherein it was said that a man could talk to his God and hear His reply. The three were John, the High Priest, Abel, the Chief Layman, and Luke, their guide and baggage-handler. It had been deemed by the king that the High Priest should make this pilgrimage to learn whether God approved of the King and of the Church. John had argued that the mission was not needed since the King was all powerful, which was a sign that God did approve. John had never truly believed the stories of the temple. After all, would not God rather inhabit the grand temples of the capitol city instead of an out of the way temple lost in the mountains?

Yet, the King had been adamant. He had seen the seed of revolution among his people and had seen their lack of spirit and enthusiasm toward their church. Recently, the image of God had come to him in a dream, and commanded him to send the High Priest to the temple. As it was said, so shall it be done.

The three rode their horses north toward the mountains with the pack horses close behind. They rode for three days. Each evening when they would stop for the night, Luke would bed down their horses, pitch the tents, and prepare the dinner. The High Priest and the Chief Layman would open their religious texts to read and pray.

It seemed that Luke had the better task as he dearly loved to cook and to be responsible for the camp. Meanwhile, John would talk to Abel about the futility of their journey. Surely, the King could not believe the fables about a mountain temple wherein God would speak to people? Perhaps it was just a ploy to get the High Priest out of town so that another could be appointed. After all, the relationship between the King and the High Priest was not as close as it had been. Abel doubted this. The people of the land were God-fearing and would not stand such an act by a secular authority. The reassurance made John feel better. Then Luke would feed them with a rich stew, or roasted meat with fresh vegetables, and they would all relax, and sleep well.

At the first sign of morning, Luke would arise and make a hearty breakfast. While the others ate, he would break camp and load the horses. Then off they would go, ever more northward.

At the end of the first three days, they came upon the first village of the mountain people. The mountain folk were very peaceful and welcomed the trio warmly. Luke told his traveling companions that he too was from the mountains, but his village was much further north, closer to the temple. The people of the village offered them lodging and a warm meal, which was happily accepted. A soft bed after three nights in a bedroll was too good to pass up. All of the villagers ate with the travelers, and the meal became a festive occasion, as they were honored by the presence of such auspicious guests. The wine flowed freely and folk dancers swirled about the party.

As it grew late, John, Abel and Luke returned to their inn. John asked that they join him for a drink and they happily agreed. In the quiet of the bar, Abel asked Luke about the village from which he came. Between sips of brandy, Luke recounted his memories of his village at the base of the tallest mountain in the land. Yes, he had been to the mysterious temple several times and had heard what he was told was the voice of God. But at the time, he was young, and he and his family moved to the capitol when he was just eight years old. He still believed the legend and was excited for the opportunity to revisit the temple after so many years.

The talk of the temple upset John, as he knew this to be superstition. Not wanting to cause any friction, he excused himself and left for his room to retire for the night. As he walked away, his mind was reeling with thoughts of this wasted trip and the silliness of the old legends.

Abel was fascinated by the stories, whether true or legend, and asked Luke to continue his childhood stories. Abel was not from the mountains, but had always been curious about the strange beliefs and lifestyle of the mountain people. Luke did not disappoint him, speaking of the heights. Luke talked about the snowy peaks where no man had ever been, and of the strange animals and plants that inhabited the land. There were trees many hundreds of feet tall and sheep that walked more nimbly on the barren rock outcrops than a man can walk across a marble floor. The villages were like extended families, and every man was equal with every other. All the people helped and loved each other, and life was good.

As the two returned to their rooms for the night, Abel was mesmerized by the tales he had heard. Surely, the mountains are a magic place. Whether the legends are true remains to be seen, but surely, God is in this place and the King was right to send us here, he thought.

The men moved further north in the morning, ever higher into the mountains. Luckily for the group, the mountain villages were spaced so that they could stop in one each night. Their bedrolls and tents remained packed and unused. At each village, the reception was as warm as the first, and the food and drink seemed even better as they progressed.

Remembrances

At each village, all the people would get together to warmly welcome their guests with a dinner of hearty meats and vegetables, followed by a celebration with wine and dancing. Luke felt wonderful to be home again, while John and Abel began to love the mountain folk more and more for their graciousness and hospitality. Each evening, after the festival, the three would drink together in the bar at their inn. When Luke had finished with the story of his childhood, Abel offered to reciprocate with his life story. John listened carefully and enjoyed the company, but was still concerned about the trip and pondered what would happen when they reached the mystical temple.

Abel told them that he was born into the home of a wealthy land baron. His family owned tens of thousands of acres of prime land and had several estates throughout the country. Early in life, he had been told that he would eventually carry the responsibility for the family holdings, and that his life would be that of power, influence and politics. Throughout his childhood, he was raised at the estate at Land's End, in the southern most region of the country. He was educated by the best tutors his family could find and spent most of his time in the company of the servants who ran the estate. His father, Count Edward was frequently away, visiting other properties, conducting business and meeting with the King's ministers in the capitol. His mother, Countess Elaine, traveled as well, managing the various estates and keeping close to the Queen in order to secure the family's reputation with the King. At the age of twelve, Abel was sent away to the King's Military Academy in the capitol for the remainder of his education.

It took another three days of traveling, enjoying village festivals, and talking into the late evenings at local inns for Abel to complete his story. Now, they were only a few days from the village where Luke had been born, and the temple. Over brandy at the end of the festival, Abel confided in John and Luke that he regretted that his life had not been as loving and satisfying as Luke's. John chastised him and reminded him that he was a very important man in the kingdom while Luke as a simple servant. Surely Abel didn't want to give up all his power and wealth for Luke's simple life? That was absurd to John.

Abel told John that he was right, but deep in his heart he was beginning to realize that Luke actually had a better life. After all, he enjoyed his work, was content with himself and with his life, and did not have to endure the ranting of the King or the ego of the High Priest. That night, Abel had his best night's rest in years.

The next morning, they continued north and higher still. Abel stopped the caravan abruptly and dismounted his horse. He ran out into the forest as the others tried to follow. There, under a massive two hundred foot tall tree, he had found a patch of bright blue flowers, unlike anything he had seen in his life. As Luke reached him, Abel grabbed his shoulder and asked him about the odd blooms. Luke told them that these were rare flowers that told the passerby that good fortune awaited them on their journey. John was confused and asked whether one had to see the flowers for the luck or whether their presence was enough.

Luke told him that the flowers were like the temple itself. The voice of God is there for those willing to hear. The flowers and the luck they bring are here for those who are willing to see. Abel smiled broadly. John was still confused. Luke told them that they must expect good luck if they wish to encounter it, and they must expect the voice of God if they intend to hear it. Abel replied that he expected to have more good luck. John shrugged and began to walk back to his horse.

As the sun started to set, the group approached the next village. Luke was the first to notice the iridescent glow and smiled. Abel and John were awestruck to see a huge field of blue flowers between them and the town's edge.

During their dinner, John asked the town chieftain about the flowers. The chief recanted the same good fortune story as had Luke, and was also astonished at the new field south of town. He had never seen such a large field of the rare flowers. Surely, his village must be especially blessed. He also advised them that the next village was two days travel to the north, and that they would need to get their bedrolls ready for a frigid night in the high mountains. Noticing that their bedrolls were for the warmer temperatures of the lower valleys, he offered them heavy goose down sleeping bags, which were gratefully accepted.

As had become their practice, the three stopped again at the bar in their hotel for a brandy after dinner. John was still confused about the story of the flowers, and deeply concerned about what could lie ahead in such a strange land. Luke told them that no real dangers existed from here to the temple, but strange things had been known to happen. The strangest of all were the sightings of unicorns. All three men had heard of the legends of unicorns since their childhoods, and knew them to be just that, legends. Luke told them that was why a unicorn sighting was such a strong omen. But John and Abel just laughed it off. His inhibitions loosened by the brandy, John then began to tell his life story.

John had been born to a poor family that lived in the slums of the great capitol city. His family had always been servants to the government officials, and it seemed that John would follow in the tradition. When he was twelve, he was made servant to the High Priest. John resented everything about his life then. He was a servant, serving those who had kept his family and friends in poverty for generations. Then, when he was fifteen, he met Don Robert, the leader of the rebels who had been trying to depose King William. He spent every free minute talking to and working with Don Robert, knowing that his actions could someday free his people, or end his own miserable life.

As time passed, the King grew old and ill, and after a final brief bout of the flu, he passed away. The King's only son was a four year old child, and High Priest Phillip was made regent. Recalling those days sent a shudder through Abel's entire body, as he remembered the reign of terror that followed. The child King was placed under house arrest, for his own "safety". Over the first few months, the rest of the royal family was exiled or killed. Six months after being named regent, Phillip declared a new Kingdom of God, to be ruled by him, and had the child King exiled.

Luke recalled hearing of these events when he was a child, but living in the mountains, he was isolated from the events on the low lands. The religious empire had enough trouble governing there, and King Phillip had little desire to waste valuable resources on the scattered mountain people. At that time, Abel spent all his time maintaining a low profile. He pledged allegiance to King Phillip, but remained far from the capitol in his own lands. He knew nothing of the specific events, which were hidden in the palaces and temples of the land.

Don Robert, the rebel leader, moved to the southern forests when Phillip came to power. He left John to be his eyes and ears in the palace to watch for a time when revolution could be launched. Due to his good service, John was promoted time and again, until he was at last made Chief Layman, manager of city affairs and scheduler of the imperial court. John knew that he had to fulfill his duties carefully in order to keep his head attached under the watchful eye of the King and his Cabinet of Bishops.

King Phillip enjoyed his newfound position. In order to properly adorn his palaces and temples, he raised taxes again and again.

Remembrances

When there were complaints and even riots, he would send troops to quickly bring those regions back into control. The King called these attacks royal inquisitions. After several years of higher taxes and rising resentment, the large land owners formed a syndicate and refused to pay taxes or to recognize King Phillip as their liege, calling for the recall of the exiled child King. This insurrection drove the King to near madness. He assembled all of his armies and made John the commanding general. He was ordered to go south and smash the rabble and confiscate their possessions and lands.

At the same time, Don Robert and his agents had been meeting with the land owners and others who were suffering under the oppression of King Phillip. He convinced them that the King must be deposed. It was Don Robert who suggested the syndicate to Abel and the others and convinced them to stop paying taxes. He warned them that the reprisal from the King would be terrible, and they should assemble their own troops, join with him and be prepared. It took five years of rising taxes and local inquisitions to finally get all of the land owners to join.

John led his massive army south from the capitol city. His staff told him it would take five days to reach the rebellious lands. That was not nearly enough time to figure out what to do then. He obviously couldn't attack his friend Don Robert. Many of the troops were loyal to the King, and would fight and die to preserve the Kingdom of God. The mass of nearly ten thousand soldiers moved south quickly along the broad paved avenues near the capitol. From personal experience, John knew they would slow down when they reach the narrower, unpaved roads that covered most of the land. How could he and Don Robert survive and perhaps even succeed in their mission to free the land from tyranny?

John recalled that after the first night, he was told that almost five hundred soldiers had deserted. Perhaps the soldiers were not as loyal as he had thought? Each day, a similar number quit the force, presumably as they passed through the lands where they were raised. High Bishop Albert accompanied the march southward. As he rode alongside John, he told him that order must be maintained and the desertions must stop. He demanded that John send a brigade of troops into the surrounding villages to bring back any deserters. John was able to convince him that any troops who volunteered for such a campaign would likely join their brothers in the desertion, and there would be even fewer soldiers for the battle.

At the end of the fifth day of marching, the army reached the edge of the great oak forest that marked the end of the King's personal lands and those of the various large land owners. The force, now down to about six thousand, set up camp inside the forest. A large meal was prepared by the cooking crew, guards were positioned, and the men settled down for their last night of peace. John sat in his tent with his generals and the tension was thick in the air. Many officers had deserted along with their troops. John told them he was aghast, although he was inwardly happy to have fewer men to battle his friend Don Robert.

In the middle of the night, John felt someone enter his tent. As he reached for his pistol, he heard the hushed voice of Don Robert. They spoke in whispers about a plan for the morning. Don Robert told him how his own people within the army had been leading the desertions and that most of those troops had joined his army, now twelve thousand strong. They embraced, and Don Robert slipped back into the woods.

In the morning, the army was down to five thousand five hundred men. They packed up and headed further south. High Bishop Albert rode up to John and regaled him again about the desertions. He threatened to take command from him and lead the army himself. John told him to get to the back of the army with the cooks and leave the battle to men. When they reached the southern edge of the forest, they saw a small group of men on horseback with a white flag several hundred yards away. John sent the High Bishop and four of his generals to speak to the men.

When the men returned an hour later, they were shaken. High Bishop Albert was shivering in fear. He told John that Don Robert had over twelve thousand troops and had completely surrounded their army. They demanded an immediate surrender, or they would kill them all without hesitation or remorse. They pointed out their own troops in every direction, and their men all shouted out and brandished their artillery and rifles. Don Robert had offered to allow any of them to join him in his march on the capitol. John asked for advice from his generals and the High Bishop. They all voted for surrender. John sent his generals to discuss options with their officers and troops who were also nervous from waiting and hearing the shouting from the enemy.

That was the end of the war. All the soldiers piled their weapons and marched into the field in surrender. Don Robert rode his horse up to John, accepted the surrender and gratefully welcomed John and all of his men into his army. John was made the supreme commander of Don Robert's troops. He sent High Bishop Albert and his priest back to the capitol to advise King Phillip what had happened. For the next two days, the troops worked together on tactics and had a large celebration each night. Then they began their march northward.

Contrary to the trip south, moving northward, more and more joined the army every day. Villagers came out and offered food, drink and other trinkets to their liberators. By the time they reached the broad paved avenues near the capitol, there were more than twenty thousand soldiers. The small force protecting the city surrendered quickly once they knew John and Don Robert were leading the force. High Bishop Albert came to them and told them that the King was dead. Knowing what had happened, he knew he had lost all, and took poison. John told Luke and Abel that he felt free for the first time in his life in that one brief moment, and cried for his people and for himself.

John cried again that night in the inn with the two men. He then told them how the new King, Don Robert, named him to be the new High Priest. From that day, John had spent his life rebuilding the reputation of the church. While there had been peace in the land for the ten years since Don Robert became King, there was growing frustration from the people. They wanted more from their religion, which had become too political and ritualistic. They also wanted more freedom in their lives, and felt the church was not doing enough to reduce the power of the government through its close bond with the King. That was why the King had sent his High Priest to the mountains and the temple. That night, John slept better than he had slept before, the weight of his past lifted from his shoulders.

In the morning, the trio headed north again after a last hot, hearty meal. The air was quite cool, and the ground was becoming barren and rocky. Somehow the trees grew taller here, as high as five hundred feet, seemingly dwarfing the mountains that they stood upon. They crossed a bright bubbly creek and noticed blue petals being swept along in the swift current. Luke smiled at yet another sign of good luck. Much of the landscape was now barren rock and gravel, with small patches of moss and lichen. They continued northward.

They stopped for lunch in a small barren clearing high in the pass between two massive, craggy peaks. Luke busily cooked some food while John and Abel set up a spot to eat. Luke was glad for their help, as they had become quite close on this remarkable journey. They sat quietly eating their meal with little talk, as they needed to continue forward as soon as possible. John heard a noise in the distance and looked up, promptly dropping his fork to the ground. Some one hundred yards ahead, at the edge of the forest was a large white horse with what appeared to be a single horn rising from its forehead. When Abel and Luke noticed John's reaction, they quickly followed his eyes and saw the rump of the beast heading quickly into the woods.

John told them what he thought he saw, but quickly thought better and said that his eyes must be playing tricks on him. Unicorns were the things of legend and could not possibly exist. Luke exclaimed that he hoped it had been a unicorn. Not only were these creatures incredibly rare, but seeing one was a strong omen of great fortune yet to come. In his entire life, Luke had never known anyone who had seen one, and his family and friends had lived in these heights for many generations. There were of course stories of a second cousin, or other distant relative would was said to have seen one, but Luke had never heard a direct account of a sighting. Luke was confident that great fortune was headed their way, and smiled contentedly while he gathered the equipment and packed it on to one of the horses.

Having passed through the summit pass, they dropped into a small valley where they would make their camp for the night. The ground was grassy here, and a large stream moved slowly through the center of the valley toward lower grounds to the west. After setting up camp, Luke gathered some greens and tubers from the nearby land and added them to the rich stew which the people from the last village had packed for them to eat. Luke was grateful for the help with dinner, which he usually had to make from scratch. As they sat to eat, John pulled a bottle of fine mountain brandy from his pouch, also a gift from the last village, and offered it to Luke and Abel. He thanked them profusely for having listened to his long story the night before. He offered thanks to God for having such good friends on this adventure. John had been through much in his life, and now felt better for having shared some of those hardships with his new friends. After draining the bottle, they built a large fire to keep the frigid night away, and slipped into their heavy sleeping bags for the night.

Abel laid there for some time, thinking about John's story and his own, while watching the bright stars visible through the clear sky above his head. He remembered that he had first met Don Robert when he had fled to the deep forests of the south. Abel had been invited to the estate of his dear friend, Lord Joseph, who was a large land owner as well. While Abel thought it was a simple friendly visit, Lord Joseph had asked Don Robert to come as well. At first, Abel was frightened that they would enrage the King and bring death and destruction upon themselves and their families. On that day, Don Robert calmed him down, and advised them to do nothing now, and that time would prove him right.

Over the course of the next few years, taxes were raised to over fifty percent, driving all of the land owners to the brink of bankruptcy. It was then that Abel had invited all of the land owners to come to his estate to meet with Lord Joseph and the rebel leader. At that meeting, the plan to boycott taxes was launched, leading to the end of King Phillip's reign of terror. That last thought brought a small smile to his face, and he fell asleep in peace.

Deep in the night, a rustling sound roused Abel. He turned over and tried to fall asleep again. Then came more sounds like walking hoofs and perhaps a soft whinny. He reached for his pistol by his side and slowly opened his eyes. He blinked. A large white unicorn stood next to him. Its eyes glowed with an eerie luminescence, like a multi-colored flashlight illuminating the darkness. It appeared to be looking directly at Abel, and he felt the light upon his face. He could have mistaken the look on the animal's face for a smile, but then it looked away. He followed its glance as it moved around the campsite illuminating at least twenty other unicorns standing about the clearing. Most of them were smaller than the one close to him, but all were dazzlingly white with the same glowing eyes and ivory horn.

Abel reached out cautiously and tried to touch the large unicorn by his side. It briefly looked at him and contentedly whinnied its approval. Satisfied that the unicorn would not attack, he called out quietly to his companions. John looked up dreamily, and quickly buried his head in this pillow in astonishment. Luke opened his eyes and his jaw dropped open in disbelief. He got to his feet and touched a unicorn close to him as if to see if it was a figment of his imagination. It was quite real and felt warm and soft to his touch. John raised his head again, and laid there slack-jawed at the scene around the campfire.

Luke jumped up from his bedroll and quickly began pulling on his clothes. He moved to the closest unicorn, grabbed it by the mane and pulled himself up onto the creature's back. In a flash, man and unicorn had disappeared into the woods. Abel and John stared into the dark forest in the area where Luke had disappeared. Finally, Abel shrugged and pulled his clothes on as well. He went to the closest animal and climbed onto its back, and off they went in the same direction. John remained hesitant, and as he stayed virtually frozen, the remaining unicorns moved slowly toward him. One very large unicorn came up on John from behind and nudged him with its nose. John flipped over shocked, and the animal moved back slightly with a small smile crossing its face. John began to rationalize the situation in his mind. Luke and Abel were gone. If he covered his head and tried to sleep, the unicorns around him may eventually leave him alone, but if they did, he would truly be alone in the cold, dark forest. If he mounted one of the animals, it would probably take him to his comrades. And if there are dangers in these woods, the unicorns are well equipped to protect him and his friends. John arose and pulled on his clothes. The large unicorn came up close to him and dropped down so he could more easily climb onto its back. John was amazed at the feeling of warmth and contentment that he felt through this huge animal. It whinnied, and off they dashed into the dark woods.

Luke kept his head down and eyes closed at first, but the movement of the unicorn made him dizzy. When he did open his eyes, he could see the forest ahead through the luminescence of the unicorn's eyes. The night air seemed warm on Luke's skin as the unicorn raced through the forest. Luke could smell the blue flowers though he could not see them. The unicorn breathed heavily as it raced forward, and under its skin, Luke could hear it whinnying in contentment. In the legends that Luke had been told as a young child, the people who were able to ride a unicorn never felt sad or wanting or alone again. He remembered that his father had always dreamed that he would see a unicorn in his life, but had to move to the city to feed his family. "This ride is for you, Dad," Luke whispered into the night.

Abel held onto the animal's mane for his life, as the tremendous unicorn seemed to be flying. It pounded the forest floor with its hooves, but the ride was as smooth as glass. He had forgotten completely about the cold as though the unicorn's body heat was providing warmth to him. The animal seemed to be like home, so warm and comforting, and it made the dark world seem a place of beauty, as it looked out upon the world with its multi-hued luminescent eyes. He remembered the legends from his youth as well. Abel smiled broadly at riding on the back of a legend, and began to laugh out loud.

John was terrified. His unicorn was flying through the woods at extreme speed, and it seemed to be totally unconcerned about that. Yet, through his fear, he felt reassured riding this enigma, this legend. None of his priests would ever believe this! They would say that he had gone completely mad! Perhaps they would be right. He could feel the animal try to comfort him with its soft whinnies and gentle pats from its tail. As he began to relax a bit, the unicorn suddenly changed direction, causing him to almost fall off. John was terrified again.

Luke was now totally confident of his mount. The unicorn seemed to be taking him on a tour of his past. He recognized several places where he had played as a boy. Out of the corner of his eye, he spotted another unicorn bearing down on him, with another rider. As the new animal joined him, he could see that John was astride it. Luke called out to John, who was immediately reassured to have one of his companions back.

Abel was relaxed and enjoying his trip immensely. The unicorn was moving smoothly and all seemed right with the world. In the distance, he saw two other unicorns and his animal quickly slipped in between the other two. Abel could see Luke on his left and John on his right. They called to each other over the hoof beats about this spectacular adventure that was happening to them. Their voices were quickly drowned out as the remaining unicorns from their camp site joined in the stampede. The way ahead was brightly lit by the luminous eyes of the twenty unicorns. All of the animals seemed to be smiling, happy to be together, and happy for their riders. Looking back, Luke noticed that their mounts and pack horses were now in the group, and somehow all of their belongings seemed to be packed onto the horses. He could not imagine how that happened, but he accepted his good fortune, and continued to enjoy his ride.

All too soon, the herd stopped at a grassy glade near a clear pool and a small waterfall. After they dismounted, the unicorns walked to the pool and drank heavily from the cool water. Luke told Abel and John that he knew this place, but couldn't be confident of the location due to the darkness. Luke went to unload the pack horses and set up the camp for the night. The unicorns, refreshed by the cool water, walked and then galloped off into the woods again, the faint glow from their eyes slowly fading into blackness. The three men were alone again with their horses, changed forever by the ride on the living legends, their now beloved unicorns.

Luke arose with the sun, knowing that they must regain their coordinates and keep moving. After walking around the surrounding area, he came back to the camp. He cooked a hot breakfast, and the smells of the coffee and sausages woke Abel and John. As they ate, they noticed that the glade where they had camped was surrounded on two sides by large stone structures and archways. Luke told them that this was the mountain temple that they had come to find. Abel and John were amazed that the unicorns had helped them complete their journey in the most remarkable way possible. After eating, they began to explore the temple.

Looking south from the glade was the forest from which the unicorns had come. To the east was a small river that flowed over the waterfall and formed the deep blue pool, and then continued southward toward lower elevations. To the north and west were large archways leading to two large stone buildings. Luke led them through the northern archway, through a small rose garden and into a small side entrance to the massive temple. The open room was quite large, roughly one hundred feet long and fifty wide. There were rough-hewn wooden pews in lines from the main entrance on the west to the altar on the east end of the building. Along both sides of the temple were small niches for private prayers or meditation by smaller groups. The large windows provided good lighting, and no artificial lights were lit, as no one else was there. The eastern wall near the altar appeared to be a natural cliff side with the rest of the structure built onto the mountain itself. Various murals were hung along the north and south sides, some religious and some natural scenes. Luke pointed out that in each work of art, a diligent eye could find either a unicorn or the blue flowers, or both. The three sat down in one niche near the door they had entered to drink in all of the grandeur and beauty of this peaceful temple.

After a few minutes, a priest entered the same door and walked to the altar, not having noticed the visitors. John immediately recognized Chief Priest Arthur, who had been running the temple for decades, far from the reaches of the capitol and the King. Arthur was born high in the mountains, like Luke, and only ventured to the lowlands when absolutely necessary. John had met Arthur once, when he traveled to the capitol to pledge his loyalty to the new High Priest. John rose quietly and walked to the altar, where he knelt next to Arthur and bowed his head. Arthur felt someone near him and looked up to see High Priest John at his side. "My Lord," he stammered, "what an honor and privilege to have you in my modest temple."

The two men rose, and John embraced Arthur. "Arthur, it is I who am honored to meet you again. Your temple is a wondrous place. Please let me introduce you to my traveling companions. And perhaps we could get a coffee?" After the introductions were made, the group left the temple and moved to the other building, which housed the Chief Priest's quarters, a school, library, cafeteria, and rooms for the other priests and nuns who served the temple. Arthur escorted the men to the cafeteria and went to the counter to get the coffee.

The other building was much less extravagant than the temple. It had plain stone walls, rough wooden tables and benches. Only one person was working behind the counter at this early hour, but gradually more and more arrived as the day progressed. Arthur returned with Bess, the cafeteria cook, along with a pot of coffee, mugs, and a plate of sweet cakes. The four men sat and savored the coffee with rich cream. John told Arthur the story of their journey and the hospitality of the villages and the beauty of the countryside. He also told the Chief Priest why the King had sent Abel and him to this place. When it seemed clear that John was leaving out some critical details, Abel spoke up about the blue flowers and riding unicorns. John seemed displeased, since the Chief Priest might think them crazy for this talk of legends.

"Yes, Sir Abel, I've heard all of that before," replied Arthur, "and much too often for me to ignore it. God moves in mysterious ways, and seems to have a plan for each of us. If seeing an unusual flower or even riding a unicorn helps us to continue on our path, and to have faith, that is a great thing." He picked up a cake and took a large bite, washing it down with the hot coffee. "Bess is the best cook in these parts," he smiled. "Thinking about these cakes helps me get out of bed on cold mornings like today."

"Yes Arthur, I agree," frowned John. "It is a true story, but even though I rode a unicorn just last night, I find it difficult to speak of." He shifted uneasily in his seat. "To be confronted by so much that has always been ridiculed as folly, and to face the fact that we don't know that much about the way the world works has been quite unsettling to me. Perhaps the King will think I've gone mad," he said nervously. "We do learn by seeing and experiencing life, I just didn't plan to learn this much. And by the way, those cakes are indeed delicious!"

Several other people had entered the cafeteria and breakfast was in full gear. Each priest who entered came to John immediately to offer their respects, which were warmly received. The Chief Priest excused himself to prepare for the ceremony. John also left, saying he needed to contemplate all that had happened. He told Abel and Luke that he would meet them in the temple in an hour for the ceremony. "Lord John did not look at all well," Luke noted, being more formal now that they were back in society, and in the sacred temple.

"No, he did not," answered Abel. "That man has been through so much in this life, and has had to fight for every bit of respect he has. Now, some wondrous things have happened, and I am afraid that he cannot readily accept them. If you have never received anything in life without a struggle, it seems hard to believe when gifts are handed to you. I have to admit that I have been dumbstruck by what has happened these days in the mountains. But it's hard to deny a unicorn when you are astride its back racing through the night."

Luke smiled. "Yes sir that is a fact. Even though I've heard of unicorns and the blue flowers all of my life, I never believed I would see them with my own two eyes. When I had to move to the capitol, I figured that it just was not my fate to see any of them in this life. I owe this experience to you and Lord John, and I thank you for that."

Abel slapped him on the back, saying "You are very welcome my friend. I am also grateful to you for helping me explore this magical country and meet so many generous people. For the rest of my life, I will remember those nights with a glass of brandy and good companionship." The two rose and walked back to the temple.

When they entered the temple, they found several hundred parishioners taking their seats in the pews. Abel recognized some of them from the villages they had visited. Many were Luke's family and friends from the closest village, where he was raised. Luke milled through the crowd, embracing many people he had not seen in many years. Two priests came to Abel and escorted him to a seat of honor in the front row. They offered him a heavily embroidered robe to wear to designate him as a special guest, and he gratefully accepted. They then went to Luke, offered him a similar robe, and escorted him to sit next to Abel. Luke was embarrassed by the gesture, as he was a simple mountain man, but accepted the gracious honor.

A line of priests entered the main entrance to begin the celebration, and all the people sat down quietly. Incense was lit, and a choir began to sing a mountain song about blue flowers and unicorns. The line of priests continued down the main aisle, chanting about the abundance of nature and devotion to God. At the end of the line came Chief Priest Arthur in his vestal robes, which were ornate with embroidery and small pearls and stones. He wore a small golden crown. As he passed each pew, he reached out to the townsfolk and shook their hands and blessed them. The people crowded to the aisle for the opportunity to be blessed.

A few steps behind him followed High Priest John, in his vestal robes which had been carefully packed for the journey, and for this particular moment. His robes were magnificent in white, with gold embroidery, large gems and pearls all about. His heavy gold crown was adorned with diamonds and emeralds, signifying his connection to God and the King. As he proceeded, he reached out to the people, like Arthur, touching and blessing them. There were audible gasps from the townsfolk as he passed by. Surely, this was a special day for their village and their temple.

The ceremony was performed as it had been for hundreds of years, with much singing and praising of God for the joys that were in their lives. The Chief Priest told the congregation about the journey of High Priest and his companions. When he spoke of the blue flowers they had seen, the entire crowd gasped. When he told them about riding unicorns, the whole room erupted in cheers. John felt himself part of that crowd and that village that day. All of them believed that what he had seen, they had seen.

Remembrances

At the end of the ceremony, Arthur announced that it was now time to listen to the voice of God. The priests opened the windows, and the breeze blew into the room, and its rushing made the oddest sound. The audience became completely silent.

Luke listened and believed as he had always believed. He heard the voice say, "Blessed are you who has shown your friends the joys of this place, these mountains, my mountains, these people, my people, these flowers, my flowers, and these unicorns, my unicorns. For you have the faith of a great man, and your faith has let you fulfill the greatest ambition of any man; to be happy and content in this life."

Seeing tears in Luke's eyes and not understanding, Abel touched his shoulder to comfort him, and seeing the joy in his eyes, Abel believed, and believing heard the voice speak to him, "Blessed are you who have fulfilled your life to the honor of your family and my church. Blessed are you who have seen and believed. My gift to you is that you will be content in your life for it is the life that I have given to you."

John saw the faces of his friends, smiling and streaked with tears, and did not understand. Being afraid, he quickly left the room and ran into the forest. He kept running as far as he could, until he could no longer see the temple. He sat heavily, and felt tears pouring from his eyes. He had come so far, had believed so deeply in his soul, but did not hear the voice. Why did this happen to him? He had single-handedly restored honor to the church after the despot King Philip, yet he was spurned now by God. Why couldn't he hear?

He wondered why he had done any of this at all. Why did he try to escape poverty? Why did he try to help his and other families escape poverty? Why did he risk his life a thousand times to depose the evil King Philip? Was it all for nothing?

Three Honorable Men

Like a quiet whisper, the voice spoke, "No. It was the greatest effort of all. You believed, and then you were seduced from me. Throughout your trials, you knew the sanctity of the church, and the depth of your faith, and made that your life's work. You did not believe for so long, through your poor childhood, and life as a slave to the evil King. You were stronger than those challenges, and did save your entire country and brought my church back to a place of honor. When you saw the miracles of my flowers and unicorns, you regained your faith in me. You do believe, and I believe in you. Do not have any doubt that I am with you, John, and I will be with you for all time."

The next morning, the trio started their journey back to the capitol. When they arrived, John told King Don Robert that all was well in the world. God was one with the people of their country, whether in the mountains of the north, the cities, or the farmland and forests of the south. The baggage-handler, the High Priest and Chief Layman remained the best of friends. Each year, they would take that journey again to the mountain temple, and ride their unicorns.

Chapter 8

Words to the Wise

Each of the following is designed to be a thought, complete and consistent for its own purpose. Together they may or may not develop a conclusion. That is not their intent. They are to be utilized at random, as their benefit is to be derived singly. To get the best benefit from these thoughts, you should quiet and clear your mind, accepting that whatever words jump from the page have a definite purpose in changing your current situation, and then to open the book, point at random, and read.

The Disclaimer

Remember that we are all fallible. Don't take these words too seriously. Extract any seed of truth, plant it in your heart, and draw your own conclusions.

You have chosen a course and are beginning along a path toward a destiny you can feel, but not yet see. Stop here, along the roadside for a moment to refresh yourself. I cannot tell you where you are going or where you have been, but only that you have reached this juncture, and are somewhat hesitant about your future course.

Fear not, look around you and see the millions of us struggling through the trials of existence toward goals which are, at best, visionary. While we may not follow the same path at every fork in the road, we move forward in the best way we can imagine.

I have decided to take this break at this time to see if any of my fellow travelers can gain from what I have seen so far. I offer you the fruits of my experience and knowledge, full well knowing them to contain only the merest morsel of nourishment; but they are all that I have, and I give them to you.

Reevaluate your path. If you have lost touch with the true meaning of life, read these words, consider every idea, accept what you believe and reject the rest. When you are ready, take my hand, and let us continue together.

For the safety of your own heart, remember the difference between love for God, love for mankind, and the love between a man and a woman. Be especially careful with the last type. Rejection by a lover will most certainly throw you off your path. Be certain that your spouse is also your best student to avoid compromising that most necessary open love for mankind.

Love is the way we survive our terror of loneliness on this crowded planet. Therefore, know that all people need the reassurance of love. Love for its own sake, and love so that others will be comforted by your love, and may decide to pass that love along to others as well.

Remember rejection does hurt. Do not become calloused with repetition. It is your duty to truly love, and if rejection is painless, then you are holding something back.

Do not be sad if your love is not immediately returned. We are all lonely and afraid of being hurt. At first, others will see your open loving as a sign of weakness or insecurity, or a clever ploy to deceive them. Be adamant! Require nothing in return for your love. Once others see the crystal nature of your gift, they will return it.

Know that some will hate you as much as you love them. Do not let this destroy you. Your success is guaranteed so long as you follow your path. Remember the thousand lifetimes you have spent preparing to face their hatred. Know that the force of your will cannot be stopped by one whose hatred has weakened his soul.

Love all children, for they are the promise of tomorrow. They will return your love and they will remember you as no others will. Be honest, caring and give all you have, for they will not disappoint you.

Remember that your material possessions will survive you, if properly maintained. This is a good thing if you can remember they are simply tools to be used along your path. Do not covet them, or hoard them, or deny them to another. We all require tools along our paths. Especially remember your duty to help others along their paths.

Remembrances

You must remain in this world, not of this world. You may feel that the life of an ascetic will move you more quickly along the path. This is wrong. As a hermit, you will come to take yourself too seriously. In this world, others will shame you out of this attitude, and your stagnation will vanish. Also, remember you must love everyone and try to help them meet their destinies.

Marvel at the beauty that is nature! It is a gift of unparalleled majesty put here to glorify our meager passage. Notice every bird, blade of grass, and especially every tree. Do not forget the beauty that is the human form. Immerse yourself in nature and breathe in its heady bouquet. Relax in its serenity, and then get back to work.

Keep the path in sharp focus. Do not allow the infinite variety of existence to drag you out of sight of the path. Once you have lost it, read and reread these words until you can see it again. Rejoice in having one more chance.

The path will occasionally pass through sad and depressing places and events. The goal is neither sad nor depressing. In fact, your destiny is Heaven itself! Therefore, accept the bad, try not to dwell on it, and move on.

Life is not fair, so do not expect it to be so. Life is a child's game which can be fun if played as a charade, or cruel if taken too seriously.

Know that your soul is infinite and will survive your body and the universe itself. Knowing that, how serious or permanent are the troubles of life? Treat life as an illusion under your control, know that it is so, and your path will become much simpler, and more fun.

Understand the eternal nature of your soul and thereby accept the tragedies in life and death. You cannot pass them off as random chance. You must cry for the victims, punish the offenders, and try to resume your path, confident that existence does not end with the acts of madmen.

When your heart is low and your friends are gone, remember that the order of the universe is a constant current through this life. It will buoy you to the surface if you have faith. Remember too how much work remains and nothing gets done while you cry.

Realize that results can be hard to see. Try to achieve happiness through giving only. When your love is reciprocated, delight in it all the more. Do not expect to be loved however. Remember that everyone is afraid of being hurt. Love and love again until you feel like an empty husk. Renew your devotion to God and the path, and you will be restored to begin again.

Examine your instinctive reactions from time to time. Is that pattern in line with your chosen path? If not, reevaluate your path. You are born with instincts, and they must certainly follow the shortest path to the goal you desire.

Take a vacation now and then. Experience the beauty of Nature and the love of family. Use your vacation to break the routine of the path for the path is not routine. If you find yourself in a rut, you have strayed. Get back on course, quickly!

Do not take the path too seriously. We have a duty in life, but we must also live. Partake of the joys of humanity to the extent that they add happiness to your life. Stop short of using the thrills of existence to escape duty.

Know that positive reinforcement abounds, and tends to be somewhat blunt. Watch for it. If you are in line with your path, you will find that you are almost shoved along it. Do not fight the current. Any stop will delay your destiny, and remember that the path is long, and life is short.

Envision the path as an extremely long gymnast's beam. All around the beam on the floor are the distractions of life, like flowers, food, lovers, and wealth. From time to time, you will forget the beam, concentrate for a moment on the wonderful things below, and fall off. That is to be expected. Always remember your work on the beam. It is too easy to lose sight of your path in the variety and richness of existence. It requires a special effort to remount the beam, and that effort will aid your future concentration.

The results of your last thousand lifetimes have shaped the destiny of this life. The events of this lifetime serve only to aid or hinder your achievement of that destiny. Do not compartmentalize your life by identifying periods between events. Instead, search for the natural progression of experiences. Analyze that trend to see if it correlates with your path. If it does not, you have strayed greatly at some point. Make certain that you have corrected this misdirection.

Forget predestination! You have chosen a destiny and a path, each of which requires work to reach and keep. Your achievement is assured only as long as you remain on the path. If you stray for too long though, you may lose them; and have to use another lifetime to reach them. Then you will be far behind schedule.

Remember the brevity of life. Also, remember that life is usually shorter for those who strive to save humanity. Therefore, use your time wisely. Do not neglect yourself either. Your goal should be to help as many as you possibly can, and have a good time doing it.

Remember that death is the logical conclusion to life, and as you have chosen your life, you have also chosen your death. Therefore, know that death will come as the final step toward your destiny in this life. As you hasten your pace along the path toward destiny, you hurry toward your own death.

Death is the natural course of human existence. It comes to all who choose this life. Yet, it is not the end, but only a brief intermission in your journey toward understanding. It gives us a chance to try a new direction. However, it should not be rushed. God has a list of accomplishments for us in each life; and only He should notify us that the mission is complete.

Do not seek to be remembered after your death. Remembrances are sweeter if they are the natural outpourings of heartfelt love. Do not worry that your memory may be short lived. The longest memories are the bad ones, and it is best to pass through life as a pane of glass, transparent, than to be remembered with hatred for even one second.

Do not take the trappings of society and business too seriously. They were created by those who have temporarily forgotten the path. But do remember two things:

1. You need to eat, so get a job.

2. It is easier to change the system from within.

Use your work to alter the system into line with your path. When your fellow travelers can understand these pages as you do, you will have succeeded.

Do not try to save the world. There is order in the universe. There is a reason for your location as you read these words. Let those in the troubled areas try to heal themselves first. You can clean up your neighborhood for starters. Once that is in good order, take your converts and move on.

In your efforts to help the world, do not hamper the progress of science, medicine and technology. God has His hand in every aspect of the universe. Seek to insure the good intentions of the scientists, doctors and technologists instead. With them on our side, success is much simpler.

Remember that everyone else is playing life as if it was true existence, so be careful in dealing with the less advanced souls in times of distress. A happy student is more receptive to his lessons. Console and love the troubled heart. When it has recovered, expose the folly of fear.

Always seek the troubled soul. Debate among enlightened souls may be delightful, but it serves no purpose other than as a holiday. An hour of loving a troubled person will move you further along your path than a thousand years of debate, or reading (even this).

Seek to emulate the Bodhisattva. As an advanced soul, the attainment of your destiny and progression toward God are assured. Others are not so fortunate. Teach them the folly of their ways and help them to find their paths. But look for other advanced souls who have come to help you find your path.

You will never achieve your goal to save mankind from itself in this lifetime. Yet, your life will still be happy and successful. In addition, you may request additional lifetimes to continue your path. Look at this as job security.

Remember all the souls you meet along the path. You may need them as you progress through future lives. Also, remember the depth of their eyes, for there you will see how advanced the soul has become.

Sometimes your cause may be best served by your absence. Watch for the signs, and know them when you see them. Do not be afraid to seek a new direction, admitting any prior real or perceived failures. It may be that you have sown the correct seeds, and must now leave the field to time and nature, and let them germinate.

Do not look for students. Remember that you chose your friends and acquaintances for this life, and they are your students. The order in the universe has placed you all together, here and now. Love one another and form a human bridge to your destinies.

When you meet enemies, look for their soul in their eyes. If you can see it, you will know that person's motivation at once. Expand on what you see. If their soul remains hidden, use camaraderie and open love to draw it out. When you have seen their soul, offer your love and understanding. If they refuse it, love them all the more for their feisty spirits.

It will help you immensely if you remember the motivation of most people is obvious, even at a first meeting. This will allow you to better determine how to teach them. As a species, we are taught to use this information for our own best interests. It requires only a slight modification to use this information for their best interests. Remember the motivation that others will see in you: your honesty and love. Also, remember that others will attempt to use you, and even use you up. Maintain a reserve, and meditate to relieve stress.

Accept your inability to teach all of your students. The requirement of your path is to teach. Your open love and logic will not appeal to everyone, no matter how kind and earnest you are.

Sleep purifies the soul. Seek to maintain the clarity of mind that you have when you awaken. This state can best be achieved through meditation. Sit comfortably, close your eyes, and push all thoughts from your mind. Allow yourself to become totally at ease before attempting to rejoin the world. With practice, you should be able to refresh the mind within a few minutes.

It is a human trait to learn from our mistakes, but not to remember our successes. We write history books about the evils of the past to make certain that they cannot be repeated. Too often, goodness is soon forgotten as not being newsworthy. Pay particular attention to the good around you so that you can learn from it as well. If you find good deeds, exalt in them, remember them, and continue passing good deeds from one person to the next.

Remember learning and growing are the true purposes of life. Each experience is a chance to learn and grow. Therefore, carry no prejudice with you on your journey. It will only inhibit your growth. Such hindrance will make your journey a waste of precious time.

Conflict is a drain of our life force. Seek to reason where at all possible, knowing that violence is the way of a madman. Remember to seek out the depth of your enemy's hatred for you, and know that there is no reasoning with madmen.

Realize the folly in exploring the limits of the physical universe. This is very important! The more a person becomes side-tracked by researching the ends of the universe, the further he will be from his own path. Given the illusory nature of existence, how beneficial can such a study be? Souls are real, the rest is distraction only.

Consider the man who lives his life wretchedly, oblivious to the cares of others, living only for material gratification. Then consider the seven billion others, of whom at least one will always be greater than the miserable wretch. A just reward: the alpha and the omega.

Consider the selfless man, whose only concern is to give. Then consider the seven billion, at least one of whom will be receptive and happier for the gift. Equal justice on earth.

Remember that the preservation of your life is not as important as the completion of your lesson. Know that you have already chosen the hour for the class bell.

Review your priorities with considerable care. Remember that only those thoughts that will follow you out of this illusion have any reality. Also, remember that the day to day trifles will dissolve for the master of his illusion.

What you consider to be your limitations are the most damning illusions. That which you fear the most will force you to adopt further illusions to defend yourself. Catalog your doubts, fears and limits, and explore their reality; in doing so, you will gradually whittle down their ranks.

Maintain a healthy sense of humor. The path is like a mountainous flight of stairs. Your destiny is at the top. The jumble of illusions that is life is at the bottom. One false step will send you plummeting to the base. Your sense of humor and your faith comprise the width of each stair. You will undoubtedly stumble many times throughout this life. Wider stairs will greatly improve your balance.

Remember God loves you and wants you to succeed. He holds you in His arms as you sleep, and holds your hand through the bitter times. When you are persecuted, He is persecuted. Remember that when you persecute another, you persecute God as well. He will not take your abuse seriously, but will chasten you just the same. Keep this in mind.

Remember you have chosen this life. Your choices have made your life what you experience today. As you must follow your path, so you must be willing to change your future (or your past) in order to remain on course. Your failure to do so will only throw you further off course, where you will be subject to all the little tragedies of life.

Remember most prophets are considered insane in their own lifetimes. Make your teachings as sugar-coated as possible. Others will improve their lives if they try to imitate you, even though they do not fully understand your motivation or message.

When you feel the crushing weight of depression, remember that ninety-nine percent of the weight comes from previous lives. As an advanced soul, you have come this way many times before. Every trouble and trauma has added a stone to the weight on your shoulders. That weight cannot be permanently removed; it is a part of you. Knowing the origin of the weight will allow you to scrutinize the cause of your current situation, and see that it is not worth the worry.

Remember nature and the universe are tools to be used in the attainment of destiny. Nature and the universe will survive you. That being so, confine your study of these things to the extent that investigation aids your path and those of your students. You may well study the infinity of inner or outer space for your entire life. However, without ever loving, that would be a tremendous waste.

Given the general confusion and insecurity concerning life and the universe, it is only natural to have some convictions and absolute beliefs in provide order to what we see. As a teacher and an advanced soul, your duty is twofold:

1. Keep your convictions to a minimum, just enough to keep sane.

2. Do not hold your convictions too dearly, as you must bend to fulfill your destiny.

Beware of excesses. Moderation allows you the time to vary your experiences. Excess clouds your judgment and leads you away from the path. Excess burdens you with doubts and problems that keep you from finding your path. Realize that those excesses will leave you at your death, so do not develop attachments to them, unless you crave the pain when they are taken away.

Know the difference between your instincts and your socialization. Remember that instincts are pure and guileless. However, the rules you have been educated to follow are the sum of a million years of human error.

Always keep your destiny in mind. Destiny is the end of your path through this lifetime. Do not confine it to specifics, but instead keep it vague and glorious. As long as you can see your destiny, you cannot become totally lost, no matter how your path winds through this existence.

Listen to music. The rhythm and melody will soothe your spirit. Pay close attention to the lyrics. How many songs are about love, utopia, or faith? Now, who truly believes that we are alone in our efforts? Especially note how many lyrics are about lost love, or man's inhumanity to man. More troubled souls in need of your help.

Be extremely cautious of your ambition to teach ultimate truth to the world. Remember that for every person who accepts your teaching, ten will envy and hate you for your knowledge. Reconsider your decision to teach at every lesson. Watch the eyes of your students, and be as certain of their motivation as you are of your own.

Some people will choose not to understand or accept your words. Watch out for them. If you encounter their resistance, just offer love and helpfulness. If you have truly met a stone wall, move on. There are many students waiting and many teachers behind you. Life is short, and duty endless.

Imagine a world in which your needs and desires are fulfilled. Imagine a world where you can learn, play, and to be with soul mates and friends. Now imagine a world of seven billion souls, each fulfilling himself according to his needs. Imagine the hustle, bustle, excitement and confusion. Look around!

Consider the child whose love is so great the he has chosen to pattern this experience after you.

In the winter of my discontent, just when all hope for salvation had faded, I found the ultimate truth. In that truth, I found deliverance from the terror of doubt.

That truth was the one strength we all can and must share to lighten the burden of uncertainty that we all carry through this life.

That truth is love. Love is eternal and as pure as the face of God Himself.

While this body must in time fade to dust, my soul will be alive in love: my love for God, and my love for you.

Chapter 9

The Lessons

Each of us learns in different ways. That is the purpose of the various sections of this book. Some will need to hear only one word of truth before they will remember why they are here. Others will read and study their entire lives and not be able to comprehend what is really going on around them.

These lessons are presented to be a study of the theory of universal unreality. We will consider whether the world around us is reality, or a creation of our minds? Are we flesh and blood organisms living a temporary existence in a cold and empty universe, or is reality somehow separate from this place? Are joyous and tragic events occurring in other cities, countries, and galaxies random and chaotic, or following a plan? Are we truly alone in our skin, or are we connected to each other in a more spiritual way?

Hopefully, we can learn about the attributes of life on Earth, and how those things reinforce the thought that the world is not so real and impersonal after all. Remember that the road to enlightenment may seem lengthy, yet the truth about life is simple. At times, we need to repeat the lessons again and again to gain clarity about the truth and its effects upon everyday life.

Lesson 1: The Haves and Have-Nots

Throughout history, the world seems to have been populated by two basic types of people. There are those who get everything they desire, whom we call the rich, the gifted, celebrities, royalty, or the lucky ones. Then there is everyone else. That second category is massive and by no means homogeneous. The contrast of choice these days is the one percent versus the ninety-nine percent. To be in the one percent in the USA, a taxpayer needs to earn over $350,000 per year. Only a fool would consider someone making $300,000 per year the same as a homeless person with no income. Yet, that is the way these lines of distinction are always drawn. Pick a group of people small enough to be bullied. If the target group is too large, they will find their voice and fight back. Also pick a group that can be seen as different enough from everyone else that those on both sides can see the distinctions.

The separation of people into elites and everyone else always tears the fabric of society. The separations can be drawn along political, entertainment, wealth, educational, scientific, religious or even academic lines. Those perceived to be elite can begin to believe that they really are special and unique. Everyone else is both fascinated by and despises them for their abundance. Political elites are the most dangerous for society since they can actually change the rules in order to maintain their grip on power. Challenging those elites can also be deadly, as they use tanks and machine guns to put down insurrection against their authority.

In a physical universe where everything you can see and touch is real, the separations are real too. All types of elites live very well off the hard work of others. They mingle in groups of fellow elites without a thought to what is going on outside of Washington, Hollywood, Harvard, Wall Street, or wherever it is that elites congregate. They pay lip service to the problems of the greater society, espousing a desire for real change, while maintaining their superior positions and lifestyles. Many believe that there really is something unique and special about their clique and themselves. Many others shun the spotlight and use their unique gifts to help others less fortunate. Since those efforts are private, these people can be hard to see, but their efforts help change the world. All of them live each day, trying to make the best for themselves and their families, hoping to find happiness, affection and a sense of security on this rock circling the Sun.

Outside of their groups, the great masses of the people work and live in virtual anonymity. The fruits of their work flow to the elite classes through taxes, donations, movie ticket and other purchases. A few of those people will find themselves in an elite category someday through talent, hard work or even dumb luck. Many will idolize and look up to the elites, while others will hate them for their snobbery, success and wealth. Many have nothing, and seek out a meager existence day to day. Many more raise families with strong moral fabric, donate time and money to those less fortunate than themselves, and try to do the right thing. All of them live each day, trying to make the best for themselves and their families, hoping to find happiness, affection and a sense of security on this rock circling the Sun.

We are not that different from one another. Many people have tremendous talents that they can share with the rest of us. Some people will start companies, providing products that we did not even know we were missing. They will hire other people, increasing the pool of folks who are now better able to help their families. Some will become actors, and perform in wonderful movies that entertain us. Some will become educators, helping our children learn and become better providers for their families in the future. Some will be doctors, providing services to keep us healthy. Some will be scientists and religious leaders who help us to understand why things work the way they do. All will pay taxes, enabling the government to provide police, fire and national security to protect us. We are inexorably connected to each other so that we can make the physical world a bit better each day.

If we look at the world around us as part of an unreal universe (one of our creation), only a small change is perspective is needed. In the physical world, man created society so that we could all work together to improve our conditions and lives on this vast and overwhelming planet. Some people had unique talents, which enabled society to improve more quickly. Some have chosen to call those people elites. The world is real; society is the creation of man. In the unreal world, society is real; the world is our creation. All of us are completely connected, directly to each other and through our personal connection to God. There is no separation between you and me. We have chosen to express ourselves through this existence in the universe we created. Each came into this life with a plan and unique talents that we chose to express in this life. Some have blossomed whether in the spotlight (elites) or the shadows, while others have not yet remembered their talents. Each faces challenges every day to happiness, just like in a real world. In the unreal world, it is in your power to change those things.

In the real world, the separation between types of people is stark and real. In the unreal world, there are those who are fulfilling their path in this life, and those who have not awoken yet. Do not believe that the elites are necessarily following a path. Many are and many are not. In the unreal world, those separations are based on the illusions of wealth, intellect and ability. We are all part of the same soul of humanity. If we could but realize that the world is our creation, and that our real life's work is about learning and enjoying the experience, those differences would have no weight. The separation we feel is not between ourselves and those with more money or prestige, it is the separation we feel from God and other souls. Just like the world, the separation is also false, if we could just see through it. Do not feel alone. Do not feel like less of a person than someone who has money or a big house. All of that is illusion. Find your connection to God and to each other. That is the real source of happiness and contentment in life.

Words to the Wise

Lesson Two: Scientific Investigation

Science and its tenets can be difficult for a beginning illusionist to deal with. We have been taught throughout our lives that science reveals the truth. Its findings are supported by experimentation under the Scientific Method, which insures their validity. These facts are hard to dispute from the vantage point of life on planet Earth. However, in this theory of absolute objectivity lies the subjectivity of science. Although the conditions of any experiment are controlled within the context of the laboratory and within guidelines based on physical existence, there is no allowance for spiritual factors. Science assumes that physical reality actually exists, and makes its judgments from there. The concepts of spirituality and physical illusion are completely ignored because they cannot be seen and measured.

Consider the student of science who does an experiment on the internal environment of his classroom. The student can test the temperature, humidity, atmospheric pressure, suspended particulate levels and so on. Conclusions could be made upon this experiment that the class room is too hot, cold or humid. Yet, this analysis is incomplete. The student may decide that the classroom is too warm and so the windows must be opened. After opening the windows, it could be found that the outside temperature is even hotter than the classroom. Other important factors should have been considered in the experiment. It was limited to the room, and the external factors were ignored. That student may well have thought he had examined all the available information. Imagine that the classroom is our universe, and the windows are opaque. We make judgments based on what we can see and measure only.

Similar conclusions are repeated daily in science. Take the work of Sir Isaac Newton, who composed the first laws of physics. For centuries, these laws were found to be absolutely true through experimentation. Science and society progressed for centuries based on the truth of these laws. Albert Einstein developed additional laws of physics in the last century. These laws were quite different from those of Newton. While Newtonian physics worked well on Earth, when the context was expanded to all of space-time, the rules had to change. Then, Max Planck, Einstein and others discovered quantum physics, which contradicted both Newtonian physics and Einstein's relativity. The context of reality changed yet once again.

This is the way of illusion, therefore the experience of science. We choose to believe that there is more scientific reality to discover, and eventually someone finds it. Whether the new reality is a quantum particle, exoplanets, or new species of plants, birds or animals, the discovery does occur. Why is that always the case?

Let us try a mental experiment for a few moments. We may assume that these scientific breakthroughs continue to occur because someone has the desire to make such a discovery. It is only possible to find these things if people want to find them, and will expend part of their life experience looking for them. Consider Einstein's theory of special relativity. The tenet is that a person cannot determine the speed and direction of an object while riding on that object. Also, a person's perception of the motion of an object is based on their own motion. None of us can feel the Earth spinning on its axis or speeding through space on its annual trip around the sun. Scientific theory states that the universe is expanding, but we cannot tell where anything is going, except in relation to ourselves.

All scientific experiments have taken place under the assumption that physical reality is the only truth, which then imposes its rules and realities upon us. A new level of understanding comes when we realize that the universe is our creation, made ever more complex by our desire to find more dimensions of reality there. If we can accept this, we can see our world a little differently. It makes sense why scientists continue to find new species of life, new astronomical phenomena, and ever smaller bits of true matter. There are so many of us living this illusion that there is a strong likelihood that many will want to expand their conception of the universe. It is those people who will spend their lives looking at their illusion through a microscope or telescope, trying to uncover another layer of reality.

Will they ever discover the last piece of the puzzle and be able to end mankind's search for truth. That is very unlikely. The universe is our toy and will continue to develop and change as we discover new things. For those people whose life goal is to search for physical truths, they have an unending resource to feed their desires. As they discover new truths, their efforts improve our lives.

The danger of science is when it becomes the only accepted truth. There are some people who believe that religion and faith are false. Science has become their religion. It is true that religion is based on faith and requires that followers accept things that cannot be proven. To non-believers, the inability to prove a religion scientifically makes it false. When science is very theoretical, those people will readily accept those concepts as fact, confident that man will eventually figure out the details. They eagerly accept concepts like dark matter and dark energy as factual, even though there is no understanding as to what they are. They will accept that those two things account for 96% of the stuff in the universe, with only mathematical equations as proof. However, they will call people of faith fools. Over time, dark matter and dark energy will be found. The universe is the scientist's toy as well. Then, future generations of scientists will be on to studying the next concept, never recognizing that all of these discoveries have occurred because people chose to spend their brief lives looking for them.

Let us use a thought experiment to understand the physical universe and the Big Bang that started it all out, according to the latest scientific understanding. I do not doubt the science on any of this, to be clear. But the story is utterly amazing. Here we sit upon the Earth, a ball of iron and rock about seven thousand miles in diameter, weighing about six thousand million, million, million tons. First, squeeze the whole planet down to the size of a grain of sand. Next add the sun and all of the planets in our solar system, and squish them into that same sand grain size bit. That is not a small task since the sun alone weighs over three hundred thousand times as much as Earth. Go ahead and add the two hundred billion suns in the Milky Way galaxy and their countless planets and nebulae. We have to squeeze really hard now to keep that one grain of sand size, but are getting there. Next, add the other two to five hundred billion galaxies in the universe, with their countless billions of stars, planets and black holes and keep squeezing to keep that same tiny size. Whew! Now we are four percent finished. We need to add twenty-five times more stuff now to account for the dark matter and dark energy in our universe. We do not know what they are yet, but they must be there to support observations, so add them too. We now have all the stuff in our universe shrunk down to the size of one grain of sand. As a final step, we need to make the grain of sand 66 trillion times smaller, so it is the size on one atomic nucleus. We have recreated the singularity (an infinitely dense piece of matter and energy) from which our universe was born.

These are the facts according to science. I personally believe it all to be true. However, it is ironic that a person can accept that as fact while telling people of faith that their beliefs are false. All of the truths of science do not disprove any religion. Those facts help reinforce the truth that this universe of ours is a truly miraculous place where unbelievable things happen and are discovered every day.

Science is a great calling for those who choose it. All of this life is part of an illusion that we have created for ourselves. Those among us who choose to test the limits of what we see around us are doing a great deal to improve all of our lives. The risk begins when we start believing that the illusion is real, and the reality of our connection to God and each other is the illusion.

Be careful dealing with atheists. All of us are free to believe whatever we want. When someone forces their beliefs on others and calls people of faith fools, they have shown themselves to be cold and intolerant. Choose instead to surround yourself with people of faith, who can readily accept the great things that science had done for us all, while still accepting that there are other truths for us to find.

Lesson Three: Desire

The desire to have more and be more has been a heavy burden on mankind for countless generations. Although we have achieved much, there are always some things that we cannot obtain. We begin to feel that we do not deserve to have them, and will have to overcome huge challenges and fight like the dickens to win them. We are taught that the most important things in life will be very difficult to obtain. We must strive, sweat and fight for them. When we believe that, we develop our own obstacles that keep us from succeeding. Have you ever noticed how difficult it is for you to obtain the things that matter most in your life? On the contrary, have you noticed how easy things that not as important are to obtain? There is a good reason for this. Throughout our lives we are taught to value certain aspects of the physical universe more than others. The list of most valued things differs greatly from nation to nation, and even from person to person. Yet, for each person, there are things that have high value.

We are taught that obtaining those valued things is much more important than all else. Since we value those things more, we try harder to get them. We like getting other stuff also, but they are not so important. This emphasis on certain things creates the stress that we feel, as we make our achievement of those things a measure of success or failure in our lives. The level of stress in our lives is the key. Our ability to succeed is inversely related to our stress level on each particular aspect of life. Those things that generate high stress levels also generate anxiety and feelings of worthlessness. This fact does not necessarily keep us from achieving them; however, it does reduce our odds for success.

We can see this by looking at those lesser desires in life. Those desires seem simple to achieve. We spend little effort and they are almost thrust upon us. We see our success as evidence that those things were not valuable, as they were easily available. Nothing could be further from the truth. Everything we crave has already been achieved by someone else. That is not because they worked harder or were more deserving. Those people did not assign a high value to that desire. To them, this thing that we value most of all was not important, and they found it easy to obtain.

We have placed our emotion and anxiety onto a desire that someone else found simple to obtain. In a universe of illusion, nothing is hard to get, unless we believe it will be difficult and allow our stress level and anxiety to swell and block us from achieving it. Virtually all of our desires are things like comfort, money, cars, toys, food and so on. When we allow our emotion and anxiety to overwhelm us, we give those desires power over us. We have made those things real.

Why are the less important things so easy to get? We do not worry ourselves. We tell ourselves "Well, if I get that thing, great, but if not, it's really no big deal." In those very words, we give ourselves permission to have them. We recognize that they are not vital, and not real. That is exactly right! None of it is real. That being said, we are living in this universe, and we need our illusions to exist here, so it is okay to have the illusions you want. However, once you try to make them as real as yourself, they dissolve and run through your fingers. As with all things in the universe, they must be themselves. Being illusions, they will all ultimately vanish.

If all things in the universe are unreal, is our desire for love and affection from another person also an illusion? If people are real, then the desire for a companion must be a desire for reality, not illusion. Why is this often the most difficult desire to fulfill? The answer is illusions. Often, the desire for companionship stems from a heartfelt desire not to be alone. That comes from our own inability to cope with the world around us.

What is this world around us? Certainly not reality! It is an illusion, a dream fabricated in the Experience Center years ago. This desire not to be alone can be restated as "I am unable to deal with this universe which I have made for myself, and must find someone to build a better one for me." This desire for love is not for the person, but for their set of illusions to replace our own. Other desires are more apparently unreal, including things like sex, money, and physical possessions. These are all based on the physical aspects of our bodies and the world around us, and are therefore unreal. They feel real because we chose to live in this universe.

What about our soul mates? We have spent many lives together, and we know that special person is out there looking for us and waiting to continue the adventure together. Do not believe that your life cannot begin until you find them. You are wrong if you feel your life is in limbo without them. You chose this life, and all of the people around you are the ones you have chosen to be here. Your soul mate will arrive when the timing is right. If you want to wait for someone else, then you are relying on them to give meaning and purpose to your life. You are waiting for a different universe to replace yours. Your life is your own. Let go of your soul mate. When you can release your anxiety and focus on making the most of your life, they will find you.

The lesson of unmet desire is about trying to make things real. Since the universe is an illusion, the desire to make things real will fail. To have a happy life, you must recognize the true nature of things. Recognize them for what they are, accept their nature, accept them and use them. Then release them as the illusions that they are.

Lesson Four: The Kingdom of God

Many people await the coming of the Kingdom of God. For many, this kingdom is seen as a physical environment of people and angels. Different faiths have varying versions of it as:

1. A kingdom in Heaven that we will all enter after we die.

2. A kingdom that will come to earth to fulfill prophecies and save us all.

3. A state of being to be strived for through the attainment of enlightenment.

Unfortunately, these views reinforce the idea that we are separate from God and have limited control for what happens in our lives.

The Kingdom of God is coming to save us all!

This belief implies that the Kingdom of God is not here yet. Since we are not part of the kingdom now, we are separate from our Creator. Our world is on its own, heading for destruction, ruin or some other calamity. The world is in disfavor with God, we are separate from Him, and therefore we have no control over the things that happen to us here and now. Earth is on a course for destruction that none of us can stop.

If I choose to believe this, then I must keep faith that God's Kingdom will come and correct all of the bad things in my life. I can try on my own, but since the bad in the world is the work of the Devil, my efforts will be wasted.

You will enter the Kingdom of God after you pass from this life.

This view is a corruption of the true course of the human soul. It formed over time to help people believe that they would survive death since they felt the depth of their minds and could not accept the end of existence. We were told that this life was a training ground for our true existence, the eternal life with God in Heaven.

Over many generations, this view has been reinterpreted. The revision became: "You will enter the Kingdom of God after you die, if you are good and do what you are told." Adding conditions to entry into God's Kingdom drove a wall between God and us. Being a creation of God and having an eternal spirit was not enough. We must conform to a code of conduct written by other men living their illusions, attempting to define God's will. Variations in what constitutes that code of conduct have led to confusion, the proliferation of sects, fear, hatred and war.

What happens if we fail to live up to the code, or live according to the wrong one? To solve that problem, we created Satan. If you cannot fulfill the code, you must be punished. Man's creation of Satan has led to even more horrors, wars, fear and agony. This viewpoint further separates us from God, because He is in Heaven and we are stuck here on earth, trying to follow a code so that we can be with Him again. This is a tragic error that has marked billions of people as sinners and bad people.

The Kingdom of Heaven is only for the Enlightened.

This view again separates us from God by putting us somewhere outside of His Kingdom. The religions that accept this tenet contend that each person must go through many lifetimes, learning and growing, until at last we are prepared to be enlightened and understand ultimate reality. This achievement is mystical and grand, and few will be able to attain it. Only the few are worthy of God. Only sorrow and misery has been gained by driving such divisions between people!

Enlightenment is seen as a method of escape from a continual process of rebirth. Each of us will be reborn for many lives of misery until we become enlightened. Only then will we be free and happy. The Kingdom of God is a place to escape from life. This common thread in all of the viewpoints has placed a heavy burden of sorrow and guilt on each of us.

We must wait helplessly for God to come and save the Earth. We must meet a code of conduct or we will be subjected to horrible suffering for eternity after we die. We need to live many lifetimes trying to learn enough to escape the misery of life. None of these is life affirming and none let us know that God does love us. In fairness, they were crafted over a very long time by well intentioned people who were trying to define our connection to God. With their understanding at the time, they tried to explain unknowable concepts to people who craved help in finding their place in God's realm. The separation between God and each of us appeared only because that was how everyone felt in their hearts.

Be clear, in the unreal universe, there is a Kingdom of God. While we live in a world of illusions, all of us and our illusions are part of God's Kingdom. Since our world is an illusion, there is no separation between God and us. God and all of our friends are with us now, close enough to feel their breath on our faces if spirits could breathe. While other concepts focus on separating us from God (He is in Heaven, we are on the Earth), in the unreal universe, there is no distance between you and God. The apparent separation is the illusion that we have created so that we can grow and experience this life. We are the Kingdom of God, and that Kingdom is here, right now, all around you.

How did we ever get so far off course? We are not stupid; our souls have always known the truth. Were we afraid? Absolutely! We have all been afraid to face the world around us from time to time. The fear comes from our failure to remember that we created the universe that we see around us. When we see it as reality, it becomes powerful and out of our control. It is so big (some 14 billion light years across) and we are tiny and insignificant. Each of those beliefs about the Kingdom of God is full of truth; it has only been our fear that added the errors. Let us look at them again through the eyes of the illusionist:

The Kingdom of God will come to save us all.

The Kingdom of God is our salvation, and it is here now! If we recognize the error of our fears, acknowledge our goodness and express the true love in our souls, then the Kingdom of God will be a true government, with leaders who lead from their faith, and followers who follow their paths, assured that the fulfillment of their destinies will help fulfill the destinies of others. Those who acknowledge the reality of existence are already fulfilling their roles as members of the Kingdom. Everyone else is also a member; they just have not realized it as yet.

There is no separation from you and God, or from you and me. We have chosen to experience this lifetime together in this set of illusions. Everything that you or I have done so far had led to this moment in time, when I am reminding you of your connection to God and to all of us. This life is a gift from God, and an opportunity for you to express your true self and let your path and your love fulfill your destiny and to help others achieve theirs.

You will enter the Kingdom of God after you die.

This is true. You will be in the Kingdom of God after you die because you are already there! Your death will not change that and you will remain in the Kingdom for all time. It was man's fear that caused him to attempt to limit entrance into God's Kingdom. This fear also led people to control others by the creation of Satan.

Science may tell you that the fear of death caused man to create God. It is true that man's fear of death does help him remember God's existence. If a man has no fear of death, does he need to remember God? Maybe not, but that is not necessarily bad. Nature is the expression of God, as defined by our chosen illusions. Nature cannot pray or burn incense, or raise massive cathedrals. Yet, nature is not damned for not conforming to a code. It thrives in infinite variety. How can that be true? God had no fear. God does not doubt our love. He has created us, and we are His children. If our experiences in this particular lifetime causes us not to praise or remember Him, that is not a problem for God. God is not jealous. Our love is a given, like a child's love for his mother. He knows we will return to Him when we rejoin Him at the end of this experience. His love for us is always there, just as a parent's love continues for the child who has gone out to play and has momentarily forgotten his family.

The Kingdom of God is only for those who are enlightened.

This philosophy has many parallels with the true course of human existence. With an understanding of illusions, it is apparent that we have already achieved enlightenment, but may not remember that right now. You can live as many lives as you choose in this earth illusion, but you do not have to be here at all if you change your mind. Enlightenment is therefore the recognition of your intimate connection to God and each of us. That connection is reality, whether you have chosen to recognize it yet or not. You are enlightened!

All of the philosophies of man contain the roots of truth, but also many false elements that we have knowingly placed there. We did that since we felt disconnected from God or not worthy of His love. If we garner the truths of each, perhaps we can come to a more accurate statement on the Kingdom of God. If we eliminate the elements of fear, separation and lack of worth, we might end up with something like this:

> We are the Kingdom of God. We are here on this Earth to express our oneness with each other and with Him. If we fail to meet our destiny, God will not be angry or punish us. The world is our illusion, and any separation it places between us and God is just another illusion. We are all one with God in love, now and forever.

Lesson Five: Patience

There is a pattern to the course of the universe. That pattern is consistent, follows the shortest path, and performs on schedule. All aspects of the physical universe flow along with the course of the universe, whether we can see or feel the motion or not. The lesson of patience is that the course of the universe (also known as Tao, or the Will of God), will fulfill itself at the correct time. No variation to the plan will occur. There is no reason to lack patience or have a short temper. Impatience accomplishes nothing, and will only force you further from your destiny.

Patience is a virtue. All opposite emotion is destructive, either of you or others. Those feelings must be caste away before they do more damage.

A person who recognizes the truth of his life, his God, and his destiny has infinite patience. The master of illusions craves nothing, hoards nothing, needs nothing, and therefore attains all things at the right time and in incredible abundance. In the recognition of your divinity is the lesson of patience. As with the lilies of the field, you only need to pursue your destiny to accomplish all things, and in doing so be rewarded by God.

Lesson Six: Fundamental duality

The major cause of anxiety, fear, and failure in this universe is the belief that some aspects of life are good and some are bad. This is the child of countless generations of people who have tried to explain their actions and lives as the result of a benevolent God and a purely evil Satan. This has led to the belief that good and bad are truly separate, and that a man must choose one over the other. The existence of goodness was seen as evidence for the existence of God; and health, wealth and happiness were deemed to be the rewards for those who worshipped Him. Those things and actions that were evil were seen as proof of existence for Satan; and sickness, poverty, and misery were penalties for those who chose the darker path in this life.

What was deemed good or evil has varied over time and from one culture to the next. The basic context remained the same: those actions that conform are good; those that do not are evil. In some cultures, for example, suicide can be an honorable act, if done for valid reasons. In the West, that same action is seen as defying God's Will. In most cultures, killing other people is deemed evil, except in war, where it becomes good. The Jains in India sweep the insects from their path to avoid killing any living thing.

Why are so many variations to the definition of good and evil? Can some religions be true, while others are false? That is not likely, given the number of people and generations of man, interpreting what we believe to be God's Law. As normal people, we are constantly asked to look for the commonality in things and events. Any religion that has been developed over the centuries cannot be totally wrong. Since all religions have been developed and refined by people, no one should believe any one is perfect.

There must be other factors at work here. That factor is duality. Duality, or Fundamental Duality, is the concept that all things have two sides. No one thing or person or event is fundamentally good or bad, right or wrong, tall or short, or limited in any other one sided way. Albert Einstein referred to this as Relativity, in speaking of space, planets and time. Native Americans believed you had to walk a mile in another man's moccasins before you could judge him. Lao Tzu said, "Good and evil are the two sides of the same coin." Einstein's theory of special relativity states that it is not possible to determine the motion of an object from the surface of another moving object. One can only compare one thing's motion relative to the other. The references are endless.

The same is true with the cultures and beliefs of people. We all were taught the inherent goodness or evil of the things and situations around us. This knowledge is part of us, and we use that to make value judgments on everything that happens to us throughout our lives. When we look at the lives of others, we surmise whether their actions conform to the beliefs we were taught, and make judgments on those people's goodness.

Nature is a gift from God, and so are the cultures of Man. They are provided in such abundance and diversity that they scream out to us that there is no good or evil, only diversity; yet we do not see it. For countless generations, people have recognized the brutality of the natural world. Charles Darwin called it "The Survival of the Fittest." We have grown to accept that as true, but we see no inherent evil in the actions of a predatory beast. We accept that the shark or lion is only fulfilling its purpose on Earth. Mosquitoes carrying malaria have killed millions of people, but no one believes that those insects are instruments of Satan. The mosquito is one of billions of species fulfilling its life cycle.

Throughout the history of mankind, we have recognized the beauty and serenity of the natural world. We have catalogued an almost endless list of species of beautiful birds and flowers and animals. We cultivate gardens and build parks in the middle of great cities. Thousands head to the countryside each year to get away from it all. We relish the time we can spend communing with Nature in all its glory. The same is true with each and every thing in Nature. Each has aspects that we deem to be good or bad. However, none is either good or bad. They just are. Each human being is the same. We just are who we are. That is it.

If we decide to declare a thing to be all good or all evil, we can be certain that somewhere on Earth, another person has deemed that same thing to be the opposite. How can that be true? Our error is in deciding what is good and what is bad. We have created a line in the sand between good and evil and have placed all things on one side or other of that line. We try to align ourselves with those things and actions we have deemed to be good, while pushing those evil things away from us.

Reality must ultimately prevail. God is neither good nor evil. God simply is. Evil does not exist for God, as God cannot conceptualize anything separate from Him. That is because there is nothing separate from God. We believe ourselves to be separate from God. This is another mistake. We do have separate forms, but we are part of the creation, and therefore part of Him. Our fears stem from our failure to remember this truth. If you could feel the hand of God on your shoulder and the closeness of the spirits of your friends around you now at this moment, you would have no fear and no doubt of their love. We are all still there in the Experience Center together. You and I chose this universe and this life. That does not change our true nature. However, we have convinced ourselves that we live in a real universe in real separate bodies. That illusion has made us feel the separation so well that we can accept other things to be separate from God, like evil and Satan.

Reality begs to differ. The universe performs on schedule. Actions occur when it is their time. Yet, no actions are inherently good or bad. They just happen. If we can release our desire to judge each person, thing and event, we can begin to see that our universe is simply moving forward along the path of God's Will (Tao). Our lives will be more joyful and powerful if we can stop fighting that flow. Your path will lead you to your destiny, and your path is in perfect alignment with God's Will.

Lesson Seven: Miracles and Disasters

It is a fact of our existence that miracles and disasters occur. There will always be debate as to the definition of a miracle, but we all know what a disaster is. We can apply the definition of disaster to miracles by only changing a few key words:

> Disaster - A sudden and violently bad occurrence which causes a high level of misery, damage and chaos.

> Miracle - A sudden and wonderfully good occurrence which cause a high level of joy, mending and contentment.

The reason to use similar wording for the definition is to show that both things are quite similar, expect for our interpretation of the outcomes. Each is unexpected, dazzling and causes a great amount of change in the experience of those affected. To us, one is bad, and the other is good. How can we compare a miracle (birth of a child) to a disaster (plane crash)? Can any good come from a disaster? Can bad arise from a miracle? This depends on our relative viewpoints of the events.

The birth of a child is the creation of new life, with all its incredible vitality and hope, and clearly a miracle. If the child is disabled, unwanted by the parents, or the result of a rape, the miracle tarnishes. A poor family with ten children and no food may view the birth as a real disaster.

How can a disaster be seen as good? Disasters vary from one to the next in degree of damage and loss of life and so on. A building burning to the ground may be beneficial if it was a breeding area for rats or otherwise too dangerous to inhabit. When one disaster occurs, it may help us find ways to prevent future occurrences.

We all view the loss of a human life as a disaster. We feel this way because:

1. Death is the termination of life and the end of the individual.

2. We all fear death, and we believe the deceased did not want to die.

3. When we die, we are gone forever.

The answers to these points rest in our faith. Too many generations have gone before us, and they told us that death is not the end, but only a new beginning. That is too little comfort to cure the pain we feel from the separation.

Our fear of death has made the fact of death a disaster. Our faith is not enough to overcome this fear. The lack of faith comes from our feeling of separation from God and from each other. If we could truly feel our connection with God and all people, we would lose our fear of death. We would recognize that death is only the end of this experience in our universe. That would be a great leap of faith for most of us.

We fear death because we are trained to fear it, and we believe it marks the end of this life which is all that we know. We do not know what will come next, if anything. We do know that no one can tell us what will happen with absolute certainty. The incidence of resurrection is pretty low, and the evidence of a next life is only in words that have no proof.

If we can accept the existence of God for a moment, then we can understand that death is no longer meaningful, just a stepping stone toward our higher enlightenment. If we can accept that our death is not an end, then we must accept that death is not bad. Just as in Nature, death is the natural order of things. As such, it is not an evil occurrence, and a disaster with the cost of human lives is no longer bad, it simply is. Clearly, we cannot turn death into a miracle, but given the existence of God, we can at least change it into something neutral and natural.

This is why the lesson on duality is so important. While death is not good, it is also not inherently bad. It just is. Death is a natural occurrence on this planet. Along with all other things and occurrences, it is not good, bad, beginning, end, or anything else.

Each aspect of life can be viewed similarly. Each thing that occurs or comes into your life is there for a reason. Each occurrence happens for your development, and to help you on your path. Included in that myriad of the aspects of Nature are you and me. We are not good or bad, tall or short, thin or fat, truthful or liars, sinners or saints. We exist in the God's universe along with every other thing.

The Old Testament states that we fell from grace when Adam and Eve consumed the fruit of the Tree of Wisdom, and then knew the difference between good and evil. We created the difference between good and evil from the mists of our own self-doubt and lack of faith. The fall from grace occurred shortly thereafter, when we determined that God was good and that we were less than that. We have tried to overcome our sins for ten thousand years.

We need to remember that the universe is the creation of God, and that every aspect of it is also the creation of God, including you and me. As creations of God, no thing is good or bad, but each reflects His image. We are never separate from Him. We just fail to believe the connection. We remain unconscious of the truth that God is as multi-faceted as His creation and each one of us.

Lesson Eight: The Elements of Love

Love is the most important thing in the universe. Love proves that we are aware of greatness outside of ourselves. Being in love or feeling love in your heart is an emotion to be savored and shared. All other experiences pale in comparison. Love is a phenomenon of interpersonal relationships. It is not a possession and it cannot be held, only given away. Love exists in its transmission from one person to another. Love is not held or owned by either the giver or receiver, it is just the experience of the transfer of emotion that we call love.

What does this mean in an unreal universe? If love can only exist during its transmission from one to another, then love cannot exist without interpersonal relationships. It is all well and good to love mankind in your heart, but if no one ever receives that love, who can say it existed in the first place?

From this arises the concept of elemental love. Elemental love breaks down the emotion of love into its components. Knowing the pieces, we can better express our love in a consistent way. Consistency is critical because it insures that we are expressing our true self. If we can do that, we can be known and loved for who we truly are. Inconsistency will lead other people to see a blurry vision of us, and never really know us. If they ever love us, the love will be based on a false vision, and probably not last. Let us dig a bit deeper:

1. Love is the ultimate connection between souls in the physical universe. The universe is an illusion that we have created in order to express our true selves and fulfill our destiny. The people we see are also illusions, because what we see with our eyes are illusions that their souls have created to express their true selves. Reality exists only in the expression of our true selves, and the purest expression is love.

2. Love exists only in its expression. All emotions are internal to your body. Their existence is only made real by their expression. Love held inside can never be realized. It must be expressed to others in order to become real.

3. Love must be consistently expressed. If we are to be judged and loved for our true selves, then that truth must be evident to others. The evidence that we provide is the expression of our emotions. Love is the most important of those expressions. If our expression is not consistent, others may not see our true selves, and have an incorrect image of us. It becomes impossible for them to truly love us, as they do not know who we are.

If we want others to love us for our true selves, the need for consistency grows. What are the elements of love? The answers are difficult, as love varies from person to person and from relationship to relationship. The basic elements remain the same: concern, commitment, sacrifice and faith. These elements start our path to love.

The Expression of Love: Level of Concern

The root of the flower of love is concern. Love's extent is measured by the extent of concern that we feel for the one we love. Concern is our interest in the situation (happy, sad, good, or bad) of the other. To the extent that we are concerned with what is happening in the life of another, we love that person. The first measure of your love is your level of concern. Examine it closely in each of your relationships, including your relationship with God. How much time do you spend worrying or thinking about the person? Do you feel sorry for them? Can you ever stop thinking about them? Once you are clear on that, you can move on.

The Expression of Love: Level of Commitment

The stem of the flower is commitment. Love can only grow from its root if you are willing to commit yourself to helping to resolve the issues or situations that face the one you love. That level of commitment is the measure of your other orientation. Other orientation is your ability to divert your attention from your own life and focus your commitment on another person. The stem will grow to the same extent that you are willing to help someone else without regard to your personal situation. This diversion can lead to many problems, but also leads you to the next step.

The Expression of Love: Level of Sacrifice

The flower bud of love is sacrifice. Our ability to sacrifice the concerns in our lives, and instead resolve the issues and concerns of another will determine the size of our flower of love. Sacrifice is the most difficult element of love and the most often forgotten. Without it, the plant becomes a weed, without purpose, and will eventually wither away and die.

The universe we see is an illusion that we have created that is full of distractions. These distractions were placed here by us and the countless generations that have preceded us. We created these things as happiness was elusive, and we felt that these things would allow us to be happy at last. We forgot that happiness was already within us if we would just open our hearts. We focused so much on the illusions that we could not see reality. We became so busy that we hardly had time to take care of ourselves and our stuff, no less help someone else. We have become deaf, dumb and blind to everything outside our own lives. With so much confusion, it is no wonder that we do not wish to sacrifice for

another. We believe that if we forget our own lives for even a moment, we will be swallowed up by the distractions around us.
The truth is that our lives are not that bad. We all have problems related to work, health and family, but these are not of life-and-death importance. Every day we are engulfed with stories about the tragic lives of others; people with no hope for the future. Surely our lot is not so bad? No life ever gets better until we decide to help. We need to constantly remind ourselves that love is what we all want, and love can only express itself with personal sacrifice. With love and sacrifice, all things are possible; without them, nothing. The level of sacrifice that we express is the measure of the depth of our love. While the expression of love is different toward spouse, children, friends, neighbors and God, the depth of that love is still based on the level of sacrifice that we are willing to make.

The different elements of love are consistent and intertwined with one another. The level of sacrifice you will make is dependent on the level of commitment you have to helping your loved ones resolve their issues. That level of commitment is dependent on the level of concern you feel for them and their problems. The final element is not so dependent on the others, but is totally dependent on you.

The Expression of Love: Level of Faith

Your faith is the sunshine, the rain, and the fertilizer for the flower of love. Faith is your belief that the concern, commitment and sacrifice are justified. For love to be strong, that faith must permeate your soul and your heart. Faith is a key ingredient in the elements of love, as your faith will allow you to demonstrate the needed levels of concern, commitment and sacrifice. With faith, love is a foregone conclusion. Without it, love will wither and die as our fears, doubt and personal problems consume and destroy it. On that day, when God, the gardener, comes to examine the flower of love that you created, with concern, commitment, sacrifice and faith, the flower will dazzle His eyes, and will live on forever.

Lesson Nine: Cause and Effect

Too often, we forget the truth of the universal law of cause and effect. This truth exists in the physical universe as well as in the world of illusions, though we ignore it in our everyday lives. In physics, the law of cause and effect states that for every action there is an equal and opposite reaction. While this may not be obvious in our interpersonal relationships, it is there. In the discussion about duality and Einstein's Theory of Special Relativity, we noted that our perception of what is happening is prejudiced by our perspective. In other words, in our interpersonal relationships, our perception of our own actions and our perception of others' reactions are skewed by our perceived position relative to others.

The lack of trust and understanding that pervades our world is evidence of this truth. If we could truly understand the actions and reactions of others, all of our inhumanities, like war, murder, and crime would disappear. Those terrible outcomes are the results of lack of trust and understanding. They are born from our fear that others may not react the way that we wish them to react. This fear is the result of our failure to understand the principle of cause and effect. How does cause and effect impact interpersonal relationships?

Every cause has its effect. Every action or inaction will have an effect on those around us. While we are not responsible for how others react to our actions, we are responsible for the effect of their reactions on us. Other people will react to what we do. Their reaction may have a happy or sad effect upon them, and that is their choice. Their reaction may have a happy or sad effect on us, and we are responsible for that. It is important that we always examine our actions and reactions to others. While they will choose how they feel, we must accept that their reaction may be unpleasant to us.

If we are unable to accept the cruel reactions of others, then we must not act cruelly ourselves. If we are unable to fight, then we should not throw the first punch. If we are not able to cope with insulting remarks, then we should not insult others. If we are afraid of being alone, then we should not push others away. The list is endless.

We have been talking so far about the avoidance of actions which others may find offensive and then retaliate. Just as this is true, the opposite is also true. If we want a certain reaction from another, then we must act that way toward them. We must recognize that each of our positive actions is having an effect, even if it is not immediately apparent. To succeed, we need to be patient and consistent.

Patience is the art of the master of illusion, while less advanced souls need more immediate gratification. Most of us do not have enough faith to fill the voids between the reactions of others. We have been taught that we need to fight long and hard to obtain the things we desire (unrequited desires). We will only allow ourselves to have those things when we think we have worked hard enough, or when our desire begins to wane.

When we begin to act toward others in the way we would like to have them act toward us, we will likely enter a period when our actions seem to have no effect. We cannot see those effects right away for a couple reasons. First, the other person needs time to look inwardly and come to their personal decision regarding our action. Much of their reaction may be under the surface while they consider it. Second, we cannot see small reactions because we do not feel that we deserve them. If we continue to act consistently toward them, we will at some point allow ourselves to see their reactions, and finally garner a level of satisfaction that our positive actions have been returned.

If we cannot continue, we tend to revert to our old ways, even more convinced that we do not deserve the positive reaction from the other person. This failure has consequences for us and for the other person. We reinforce our self-doubt and feelings of inadequacy. The other person is confused as to why we made that first attempt and then gave up. This can cause their self-doubt to soar as well.

The lesson of cause and effect reminds us that each action we take does have a reaction. That is the law of existence and of physics. The reactions of others may affect us. If our reaction is unpleasant, that is our own fault. If our reaction is positive, that is our decision too. Our personal responsibility is the key to the school of illusions. Keep it with you always.

The Master of illusions wears responsibility like a second skin. It is not a burden to carry as it is a part of him. It moves with him at each step and he does not notice its presence. The Master considers the reactions of others for every action he takes. His actions flow along God's Will (Tao), and he knows that the reaction will also be in line with that Will. The universe performs on schedule, and the Master is in perfect cadence. Those who understand the purpose of his actions move forward and grow with him. Those who do not are left behind, wondering where he came from and where he has gone.

Chapter 10

Our Nobility

In our entire world, there are only three types of people:

- The follower—A person who has not yet learned the nature of reality, but can grow.

- The teacher—A person who has begun to understand, and exposes the folly of fear.

- The master—A person who knows reality and fulfills his destiny.

Each of us is a unique creation of God. We have all chosen to live in this world of illusions in order to be with our friends, to learn, and to be happy. Once we arrived here (our births), the knowledge of past lives and the true nature of this universe was overwhelmed by the sensations of the physical world. We have found ourselves in a busy existence where we are surrounded by other people and physical objects that distract us from the reason we came here. We think that much of what we see around us is bad. Things like war, disease, crime, addiction, and natural disasters confront and kill people daily. The illusion is so great that we have become separate from our souls and often feel like we have lost our connection with each other and with God.

Our electronic connections like television, the Internet, and the news were intended to make us more connected to other people and our world. They have done the opposite. We have become so overwhelmed with information that our view of the world has become a random mass of sound and video bites. We cannot process it all, and we begin to see the world as this random mass of stuff. Randomness implies that there is no direction, and no true flow of God's Will to guide us. Without that connection to God and a reliance on His Will to guide us, we feel lost and alone in a harsh and hostile universe. The student of illusions must first recognize that this is happening, and then take action to correct the course of his life. We do not doubt that all of this activity is taking place. We just need to focus on the part of this crazy world that has direct implications on our lives and our path. By clearing our minds from distractions, we will begin to feel our connection to God and be drawn along the constant flow of His Will toward fulfillment of our destinies. As we move forward, we will find ourselves at three different levels in our understanding: the follower, the teacher and the master.

The Follower:

The follower follows in many ways. He believes that each happening in this universe has some impact upon him, and he must therefore catalog and understand them. He can become so preoccupied with things happening around the world that he has no time left to notice his own stagnation or misdirection. At the extreme, it is this type of person who may become so lost and feel so alone in the illusion that he may take his own life. Most followers will give control over their lives to the illusion; all the while protesting that everything that happens is outside of their control.

Most people are followers. They believe that forces outside themselves will guide their destiny, making them happy or sad. They may love God dearly, but their love is expressed only in prayers for salvation and forgiveness. The follower cannot understand why he is not happy or content in his life. This lack of understanding is turned inward, leading the follower to believe he is somehow slow or not intelligent. Once that begins, the lack of understanding and poor self-image can become self-perpetuating, each thought feeding on the prior one, until the follower has no direction left.

The follower will follow any trend that seems to lead to fulfillment, but will remain unfulfilled. He remains unfulfilled because he will not accept that his failures are his own fault. Without accepting his responsibility, he cannot conceive that his destiny is within reach, if he would just try. This person will follow the example of other followers who appear to be happier or fulfilled, but that will fail as well, as that is their path, not his.

The Teacher:

The teacher is a follower who has started down the path toward enlightenment, and is trying to help others understand the folly of their misdirection and unhappiness. The teacher may or may not believe his world is an illusion. What he has learned is that his destiny is in his own hands, and that no one else will solve his problems. The key to understanding is responsibility. Too often responsibility is twisted into something bad or burdensome. We look at our responsibilities as things that we must worry about or take care of before we can take care of ourselves.

Nothing could be further from the truth. In the illusion of this universe, we are only responsible for our own happiness. That is not as simple as it sounds. Each of our actions or reactions has ramifications. We are responsible for the effects of our actions. It is up to each of us to choose actions that will lead to our satisfaction and happiness. If they do not, then it was our fault, and we need to do something about it.

The teacher is beginning to believe this. A teacher may get a start along the path when he realizes that no one is doing him any favors, and that everything he has achieved has come from his own hard work. This sounds harsh, that the world is a terrible place and that we are each on our own, but it is not. The teacher may feel this way when he begins to understand. The world is a wonderful place, full of loving people as well as toys and desirable things of all descriptions. This entire world is blessed and full of God's Grace. However, those wonderful things cannot come to us until we ask for them and feel that we deserve them.

The teacher begins asking for and demanding the things that he wants, and is surprised when he begins to get them. Over time, the bitterness that started the teacher down this path softens as he becomes full of the richness of his life. He recognizes that his success came from his acceptance of personal responsibility, not from his anger or resentment from the past. The teacher knows then that anyone can do what he has done if they choose to do so. The teacher begins to teach.

The teaching may begin at his workplace, or with his friends and family, as he explains the concept of personal responsibility. Many will reject this message since they have heard it before. They want proof, and all the teacher has as evidence is his happiness. Even that may not be complete since the teacher is just beginning to move toward his destiny. The word is being spread in some form. As the teacher speaks, his most attentive listener is himself. His success builds upon itself.

Even though his enlightenment has begun, a teacher can easily lose his path. Since he is still learning, he will have periods of doubt. Not every action will succeed. He may allow the illusion of the universe to have some control over his life. During those times, his happiness and path can be lost in some tragedy. He may be lost from his path forever, and be a follower again. If his faith is strong, he will progress and reach his destiny.

The Master:

The master is a follower, yet he has learned to follow only the path to his destiny. Since he chose his own destiny, his path is also his choice. He follows his own lead, concerned only for the fulfillment of destiny. The master is fully aware of his actions and gladly accepts the results of those actions. He accepts them since his actions follow his path, and therefore the results of those actions are the fruits of his path and form the basis for his happiness in life. Masters are rare in this world of illusions.

Little can be known about the master, as he lives within his path. He is invisible to those who do not cross or cannot see his path. The master knows that reality is an illusion, and is invisible to those who are blinded by the complexity and confusion of their lives. While we may not see him, we know he exists. The master is the person who is fully aware of his life's direction. The master is fully content with his life and finds happiness in every aspect of the world around him. The master ignores those aspects of the illusion that are not joy-giving, and people who would try to take his joy from him. The master is complete, in and of himself, and therefore invisible to those who are trying to find reality outside of themselves.

It may sound like the master is self-centered and egotistical, but nothing could be further from the truth. The master can truly love others since he has no desire to find salvation from their actions and reactions. He only wants to be with them when it is his time to do so. The master does not desire the possessions of others since he knows the nature of the illusion, and that everything can be obtained by everyone in infinite abundance.

So, we have the three types of people: the follower, the teacher and the master. The follower is the easiest to find. He is us. Whenever we find ourselves lacking or desiring others or their possessions, we are following the illusion, attempting to find reality and salvation. The teacher is harder to find. He is who we should be. Not many are willing to accept responsibility for their lives, accept who they are, what they have, and where they are going. Fewer people still can believe that their happiness and destiny is attainable. The master is illusive. He is the version of ourselves that we doubt we can ever become. He is content with his life and believes that everything he wants is in reach. He knows God's love and desire to help him achieve his destiny. The master is so free and at peace that he is as transparent as glass to our eyes. Still, he is there, trying to teach through his example if we would only look.

You should note that there is no fourth type called a leader. One follows, teaches or has already mastered the lessons that others are trying to learn. Followers crave leadership, and without it are frequently lost. The success of each person depends on their acceptance of personal responsibility. If we look for someone else to lead us, then we give them power over us and grant some of that responsibility to them. Teachers and masters are busy fulfilling their destinies and recognize that they cannot lead us, as each person's path is different. The leaders we find are just followers like us. They know no more about reality than we do. Even if they are lucky enough to stumble along their path, that path is not ours. We can end up following some other person's path, never finding fulfillment or happiness. Leaders do not exist. This life, your life, is a personal expression of you in this unreal universe. No one can lead you because their lives are their own, and their paths are not your path. But you are not alone. Every person you know, have known, or will know chose to join you in this life, this adventure. We are all connected more closely than the skin to our bodies. God is connected to you too, through every minute of your existence. Living your life is about accepting His love and choosing to lead your own life in the way that only you can.

Chapter 11

The Course of Enlightenment

Just as the sun rises each morning in the illusion that is our universe, and follows its path across the sky, there is a course in the growth of our souls. Some say that a level of enlightenment can be achieved over lifetimes when we finally see the reality of our world and lives. In truth, we already are enlightened, but simply cannot remember or refuse to acknowledge it. Since we do know it, our realization of it should be called a remembrance; but since enlightenment is the most accepted term, we will use that word.

If we want to achieve our destiny and be truly happy, we need to try to become enlightened. Our ability to do this is great since it only involves remembering something we already know. Our resolve to do it is quite often lacking. We all want an instant reward for our actions. When that does not happen, we can become discouraged, and ultimately lose faith and give up. How can we change that and move closer to our destiny and happiness?

We were all taught to follow the examples of others. We mimic our parents, siblings and friends in order to learn. In school, we are encouraged to follow rules of conduct and get along with others. We are also told that we need to excel in class or in athletics in order to be viewed positively by other people. Societal norms press on us to get jobs and have families as we become adults. This has led to tremendous improvements in society, but what has it done for the happiness and contentment in our lives? Happiness and contentment come from fulfilling our destinies and re-establishing our connection with God.

The first step is recognizing that we do have a destiny. We are more than the flesh and bones, house, car and job that defines our daily lives. We need to look at our lives and determine whether we feel fulfilled and happy. For most of us, the answer is no. We can love our families and our possessions. We can feel joy and happiness some of the time. To the extent that we find ourselves unhappy or feel disconnected with other people and God, we are not following a path to our destiny. The second step is finding some small thing we can do to improve our contentment and happiness. It can be a very small step. In fact, the smallest steps are the best, as they do not turn our world upside down.

Once we, as followers, begin to move down the path toward our destiny, we will begin to receive in abundance from the universe. Each step will be rewarded, and we can become happier and more content than we ever thought possible. Over time, we will become increasingly aware of the failure of other people to do this same thing. We become teachers. We offer a few words of kindly advice to our friends and family. They may be grateful, and begin to make changes in their lives as well. They may scoff at our words and continue following the illusion, which is their choice. They may begin to resent our success as they become more and more mired in the illusions that have led to misery and unhappiness. They may hate us for our happiness. If we can continue to grow in spite of the anger and jealousy of others, and continue to love and teach those who hate us, we will be true teachers.

The teacher has already discovered, or remembered, the course of his life's work. His progression is the result of continued success, which comes from growing awareness of the true nature of the universe. The more he receives abundance from the universe, the more he will try to discover why things work that way. As he learns, he will continue to see others failing to achieve even the smallest victories as they desperately try to find happiness and truth outside of themselves.

At some point, the teacher may come to understand why things happen the way they do. The universe that most people cling to for truth is unreal. That is why people cannot find their happiness in the universe. It is not there. That is why the teacher can obtain so much abundance. The abundance is also not real and therefore without limit. If the teacher can continue to progress, he will realize that the abundance around him is not the source of his happiness. His happiness comes from following the path to his destiny and from his connection to other souls and to God. When the teacher is fully happy and content, and knows that the universe is here for his benefit, he may become the master.

The master has achieved his destiny: he is happy and content in his life. He knows that the course of his life and of the universe move together along the path of God's Will. He flows so effortlessly along his path that most people never see him passing by. He lives his example for others to see. While some do see him, they do not see him as advanced since he wants for nothing. The master is not concerned with the opinions of other people. He acknowledges them and evaluates them for the impact on him and his path. If they are not consistent with what he knows to be true, he lets them flow away like flotsam on the stream of Tao. The master is fully aware of God. The master knows that God loves him and is allowing him to live life in his own way. He is never separate from God, only looking at God through the prism of the illusion.

This is the course of enlightenment. We are born and taught to be followers. If we can progress and learn that we deserve to accomplish our destiny, we can be called a Student of Tao. If we can accept the abundance of the illusion and want to teach others what we have learned, we can be called a Teacher of Tao. If we can ever understand how the universe works, why all things occur, yet remain apart from the confusion of the illusion and surrender ourselves completely to our path and God, we can be called the Master of Tao.

The master teaches the students and teachers by example. The teacher learns to continue along his path. The student may learn that there is another way. The teacher teaches the students and masters by his word. The students learn how to find and begin their path. The master learns that his destiny is fulfilling itself at every word. The student teaches the masters and teachers. The teachers learn that their efforts can be worthwhile, and that the path is broad and full of travelers. The masters learn that they too can still learn and teach, and that much work remains, until at last, we are all enlightened.

Chapter 12

Lives

The Life of the Student of Tao:

The student accepts his illusion to be his own, and by doing so molds his life to fulfill his destiny. The student recognizes tradition, duty and responsibility. He complies with them to the extent that they help fulfill his destiny. The student lives honorably, loves selflessly and gives generously.

The student accepts his oneness with God, and understands that his apparent separation from God is part of the illusion. The student allows his faith to fill the voids. The student is often sidetracked by the complexity and diversity of the illusion. He consults his teachers for help when he loses his path.

The Life of the Teacher of Tao:

The teacher is a student whose generous gift is his understanding and love. The teacher recognizes the illusion of tradition, duty and responsibility, but does not shirk them. Instead, he fulfills them to ease the minds of his students.

The teacher is honorable, loving, and generous without recognizing those to be traits. The teacher knows that he is one with God, but falters from time to time. In his moments of enlightenment, he is happy to tell others about his path. He leads his life as anyone else, but moves mountains without knowing he did so.

The Life of the Master of Tao:

The master remains a teacher and a student. The master is honor, love and generosity. He and his path are one with God, and he knows that is the natural state of things. The master seeks nothing, hoards nothing and fears nothing, yet achieves all in abundance.

The master falters along his path, but finds the truth in every aspect of himself and the illusion. The master does not seek to teach, yet teaches nonetheless. The master lives his life like anyone else, and sees the mountains moved by others.

Chapter 13

Words to Consider about Tao

Words to the Student of Tao:

Never seek the path, seek yourself instead. In the expression of self is the expression of truth and Tao.

Seek nothing, and by seeking nothing attain clarity of purpose. Hoard nothing, and by hoarding nothing attain selflessness. Fear nothing, and by fearing nothing attain the vision of Tao.

Love nature, and by loving nature accept your oneness with it. Love all children, and by loving all children attain hope. Love each other, and by loving each other attain joy and contentment. Love God, and by loving God know His love for you.

Fear and faith are the opposite sides of your perception of the illusion. While faith accepts, fear rejects. While faith breeds hope, fear brings despair.

Unity is the only state of things. Separation is the result of your misconception of the state of things.

Do not seek riches, seek yourself instead, and riches will be yours in abundance.

Surrender to your faith, and then watch for the glory to be placed upon you.

Words to the Teacher of Tao:

It is better to teach by example than to utter a single word.

Do not seek students; your example will be the best advertisement.

All truth resides within us. Do not try to teach the truth, extract it from your students.

Every soul knows the truth already. Your pupils have only forgotten it temporarily.

Do not be surprised if your students know more of the Tao and truth than you.

Words to the Master of Tao:

The master never seeks the path, but always follows it. The master is his path, and the fulfillment of his life is the fulfillment of the path.

The path is the course of the universe, the Tao and the Will of God. The path never breaks, wanders or changes. It follows its course unerringly and constantly by the shortest route.

He who is in line with his path fulfills his life utterly.

Seek nothing yet achieve all. Hoard nothing yet have abundance. Fear nothing and thereby know the truth of the Tao.

Chapter 14

Closing Thoughts

You might be surprised to learn that this book was originally written more than twenty five years ago. I know it was a surprise for me. A dear friend reached out to me to reconnect after many years. We exchanged some e-mails and then met for lunch one day last year. I told her how my job had been eliminated after the company I worked for was acquired by a major multinational corporation. I had started the job search process, and given the protracted recession, I knew that it could be a long time before I found a similar position.

She asked whatever happened to the book I wrote, and I honestly did not remember writing anything. I believe my actual words were "I wrote a book?" I spent some time looking around, and found a couple copies in the house, along with rejection letters from a couple publishers. The publishing business has completely changed over this time. In those olden days, you were at the whim of a publisher. Each rejection letter (and I think I had at least three or four) was a huge wave of cold water on my ego and spirit. My ability to say what I wanted to say was totally out of my control. My friend connected me with her publisher, who graciously offered to take a look. After reading it, we all agreed that it needed some major editing. Of course, after that many years, there was no digital copy, so I had the opportunity to rewrite the entire thing, making many changes. It was quite interesting to see what a different person I was in my late twenties compared to the fifty-something that is me today.

Thankfully, modern software has great spelling and grammar checking capability. Much of the original writing also seemed clinical or too formal, like a textbook. Even though I wrote it all, I did not care for the tone anymore. I learned a lot more from this process than grammar, spelling and narrative style though. After all this time, I realized that I actually wrote this book for me. The lessons were for the attention of my future self. I hope that you agree with me that my writing is about faith and hope. God does love us; we are never separate from Him or from each other.

After twenty five years of separation from these ideas, I had become fairly immersed in my illusion. Life had been good to me though. I have no complaints. I have a beautiful wife, Aida, and grown children, Moy and Annette. We have a great house and are comfortable in our lives. Through it all though, I have been feeling isolated from God. As I warned in my own words, followers like me can be easily distracted by the depth and fullness of our illusions until we forget that those things are not real. That was me. It is a blessing and honor to be able to read this story again, and hopefully, I can maintain my closer connection to God. Of course, the connection will always be close, as close as skin on the body, but I may allow myself to forget that again. I do not want that to happen, but we are all just people, so that is always a risk. I thank God for the opportunity to understand reality again for a while.

Over my long separation from these ideas, I became interested in cosmology and quantum physics. These fields of science look at the biggest things in nature (the universe itself), and the smallest (quantum particles that form everything). I read in length about both as there are some tremendous scientists who write for consumption by normal folks like you and me. What I have learned is that the ability of people to understand their physical universe is still in its infancy. The theories that describe the big things (general relativity and cosmology) continue to be at odds with the theories that describe the minute (quantum physics). It is a rift that will likely employ many more generations of brilliant people. That does not even take string theory into account, which is one suggestion for the linkage between the two schools of thought. String theory suggests that there are nine or more physical dimensions, and potentially an infinite number of parallel universes. All of these theories exist primarily in mathematical models that are well beyond my ability to understand.

My current obsession is with dark matter and dark energy. I find it fascinating that after so many centuries of studying the physical universe, scientists are happy to report that all of the stuff in the universe, including you, me, the stars, planets, nebulae, and galaxies account for only four percent of the total. They coined the term dark matter because there is not enough matter in each galaxy to keep it from flying apart. Dark energy is the term used to describe why the expansion of the universe is still accelerating thirteen billion years after the Big Bang. Imagine a fire cracker whose explosion keeps getting faster and faster for ever.

I mention all of this now because it colors the picture about how our illusion continues to grow in depth and texture as we keep looking for more depth and texture. Every few years, we have to rewrite all of the textbooks because our fundamental knowledge changes. Marine biologists will speculate about what can lie at the lowest level of the oceans. They build a new submersible capable of reaching those depths, and voila, they find something new that challenges the previous beliefs. Biologists claim that all animal species have been cataloged. Someone travels to some remote jungle or island, and finds dozens of new species. What a great place our God has given us to play in! The game of life keeps getting more and more fun and exciting.

The game is full of pitfalls for followers like you and me. We begin to believe that our illusion is reality. If we believe that, the illusion can turn on us. When we believe that all the miseries and suffering of the world can affect us, we open the door and let them in. When we fear for our wealth, health or happiness, we accept that we could lose them. The more faith we put into this illusion, the less faith and connection we have to God. As we lose that faith, we feel more and more vulnerable to the whims of fate. Many will completely lose faith, putting all their hope and trust into a universe that is not gentle and loving. They surrender their will to the illusion that they have created and allow it to destroy them.

Have faith in God. This world is your playground. It is your tool to mold and make your life as wonderful as you want it to be. If you can keep that connection alive, then this world, this illusion, will do what you want it to do. If you lose your connection to what is truly real, then you can lose your way, and waste a tremendous opportunity to share this life with others, and to be happy. Please always remember that is the true meaning of life. You are here to learn, to be together, and most of all, to be happy and enjoy your life. God bless you.

About the Author

Karl Morgan

Karl Morgan has long been inspired by religious texts as well as current authors of philosophy, cosmology and quantum physics.

He was especially intrigued by the Taoist texts of Lao Tzu and Chuang Tzu. The works of Richard Bach helped Karl coalesce his thoughts on the nature of life. The brilliant works of Drs. Stephen Hawking, Brian Greene, and Michio Kaku helped him understand that our physical universe is still a magical and mysterious place.

In all of his study, he found more similarities than differences. Those similarities inspired him to write Remembrances.

While attending the University of Iowa, Morgan studied world religions and cultures, astronomy and classical literature along with a business curriculum. His degree led him into the corporate world of finance and accounting.

Karl lives in San Diego with his wife and their beloved puppies. Their two grown children have fled the nest and started their own adventures in life.

www.ingramcontent.com/pod-product-compliance
Lightning Source LLC
Chambersburg PA
CBHW051452290426
44109CB00016B/1718